ALY
BAIN

Best Wishes

Aly Bain

Alastair Clark.

Shetland reel
(for Aly Bain)

The fiddle bow slides and hops and dances
At a speed that should sound hectic but doesn't.
Down-bow becomes three up-bows in places
I would never have thought of, following
The jags and curves of the tune as though it were
Helicoptering at a hundred miles an hour
Along a dry-stone dyke on a humpy landscape.

Down there four fingers are capering
(How don't they get tangled?) on four thin tightropes.

The result? — a tune: a witty celebration
Of nimbleness and joy, fit to be played
In a tenement room, in a hall, in the lee
Of a Shetland peat stack where the Aurora
Remembers its other name, the Merry Dancers.

— Norman

A poem by Norman MacCaig written for Aly on his fortieth birthday. The party was great, too

ALY · BAIN

FIDDLER ON THE LOOSE

ALASTAIR CLARK

MAINSTREAM
PUBLISHING

EDINBURGH AND LONDON

First published in Great Britain in 1993 by
MAINSTREAM PUBLISHING COMPANY
(EDINBURGH) LTD
7 Albany Street
Edinburgh EH1 3UG

ISBN 1 85158 431 5

A catalogue record for this book is available from the British
Library

Typeset in Great Britain by Saxon Graphics Ltd, Derby
Printed in Italy by New Interlitho, Milan

CONTENTS

ACKNOWLEDGMENTS

Grateful thanks to the following:

Billy Connolly, Mike Whellans, Phil Cunningham, Loudon Wainwright III, Dave Richardson, Cathal McConnell, Willie Johnson, Owen Hand, Violet Tulloch, Finbar Furey, Mike Alexander, Malcolm Green and Duncan Lunan, who all took time out to sit down and talk about Aly Bain and his music;

Norman MacCaig, for permission to reproduce his poem *Shetland Reel*;

Liz Wright, who could always see the light at the end of the tunnel, and who helped us in many ways to reach it;

Danny Kyle, Philip Woyka, Ian Wright and George Thomson, for their help;

Sandra, for her patience and encouragement;

All of those who rallied magnificently to the call for photographs:

Rod Stein, Bruce Spence, Dennis Coutts, Anne Bain, Stanley Sinclair, Mike Whellans, Pelicula Films, Robert Shearer, Dave Richardson, Wilma Robertson, Duncan Maclennan, Ken Roberts, Peter Cooke, Douglas Bentley, Lucy Bain, the School of Scottish Studies, *The Scotsman*, and the *Press & Journal*.

ALASTAIR CLARK and ALY BAIN

Chapter One

SOUND-CHECK

Who knows what might have happened to the scrawny, stammery, fresh-faced young Shetlander with the Elvis Presley hairstyle, winkle-picker shoes and Fair Isle sweater if he had passed that audition for *The Lex McLean Show* in Glasgow in '68?

Raw and naïve though he was, it's hard to imagine that he would have allowed himself to be sucked into the couthy kilted clique which ruled the world of Scottish entertainment at the time. More probably – and this is the worst scenario – he would have survived a few nights at the bottom of the Pavilion Theatre bill, kitted out in some garish, Brigadoon tartan, before realising that he couldn't sell his musical soul – not even for the £75 a week that was on offer. Then he would have packed his bags for a miserable flight back home to Lerwick, there to spend the rest of his days to be known forever as the useful joiner who almost made it in showbusiness.

They asked him to play *Delilah*.

He had never played it before, but he took out his fiddle and bashed out the tune as best he could from the memory of hearing the Tom Jones record on the radio a few times. The weary producer of *The Lex McLean Show* was not impressed. After the first few bars, his pen was already itching to obliterate the name of Alistair Bain from the sheet in front of him. It had been a long day, and doubtless MacPherson the Haggis Juggler was still waiting in the wings with the Whistling Postie from Glendevon. He waved *Delilah* to a premature and merciful close.

'Is there anything else you can play?' he asked.

Aly perked up a bit. 'Do you fancy some Shetland reels?' he said.

No, the producer did not want to hear any Shetland reels. But he wasn't quite finished yet.

'Tell me, Mr Bain,' he said. 'What's that thing strapped to your fiddle case?'

Perhaps he hoped it was a ukelele or some other tinkly instrument upon which *Delilah* could be brought to ravishing musical life in Aly's hands.

'It's a salmon,' said the fiddler. 'A beautiful nine-pounder. I caught it yesterday morning before I left Shetland.'

For a brief moment, the pen hovered while the producer contemplated the promotional possibilities of The Fiddling Fisherman. It didn't take long. Aly Bain's theatrical career was over before it had even begun.

Aly went away puzzled and dismayed, reckoning that if *The Lex McLean Show*, that most Scottish of theatrical institutions, didn't want to hear his Shetland reels, then nobody did.

How wrong he was. What Aly didn't realise at the time was that a huge and hungry audience awaited him elsewhere – in the folk clubs and festivals that were springing up all over Scotland as the folk revival gathered momentum on the phenomenal '60s tide of alternative culture.

Aly discovered the folk scene – and the folk scene discovered Aly – through the late Arthur Argo, a folklorist, singer and unbridled enthusiast who was a proud descendant of Gavin Greig, renowned for his collection of traditional ballads. Greig's musical passion clearly ran thick in Arthur's blood. He certainly knew a great fiddler when he heard one. And he knew, when he heard Aly Bain playing as a teenager in Shetland, that here was perhaps one of the greatest of them all.

It was Arthur Argo who persuaded Aly to leave the islands. And it was Arthur Argo who opened his door in Edinburgh, not long after the abortive Glasgow audition, to find a disconsolate Aly standing there with fiddle case in hand. It was somewhat akin to an avid stamp-collector picking up his mail one morning and discovering an envelope with a Penny Black stuck on it.

Argo had a job with the BBC, but in his spare time he had set up a small booking agency to feed the increasing demands of the folk clubs. Business was beginning to boom. He was already handling Glasgow's banjo-playing comic bombshell, Billy Connolly, as well as a young lass with a bonny voice, Barbara Dickson.

Using all his powers of persuasion – and several large shots of his favourite malt whisky – Argo got Aly to agree, reluctantly, to take a spot at the Irvine Folk Festival in Ayrshire. It was there that a remarkable musical career was launched. It was there that Aly Bain found, as he puts it, his niche in life. And it was there that a kind of one-man crusade began. The task: to put traditional music, especially fiddle music, back into its rightful place in the public domain, where it could he heard, enjoyed and played.

Arthur Argo was taking a bit of a gamble. Aly Bain was something that hadn't been tried on the folk circuit before – a solo instrumentalist, and an extraordinarily talented one at that. Up until then, the Scottish scene had been dominated by songs and singers, ranging from exuberant, macho groups of the type immortalised by Connolly as 'four Aran pullovers singing *The Wild Rover*', to gloomy contemporary songwriters, hunched over blues-soaked acoustic guitars.

The folk fans at Irvine that summer could hardly have been aware that Aly Bain was a messenger heralding a new era which would ultimately see the singers toppled from their bill-topping perches by a swarm of predominantly instrumental, rather than vocal, groups.

As Owen Hand, one of the top Scots singers at the time, recalls: 'Aly was the first person to come into the Scottish folk scene with a traditional instrument and a high degree of expertise. Musicians of his quality just hadn't been heard before.'

Billy Connolly, too, vividly remembers being 'blown away' by his first taste of

Arthur Argo recording singer Jimmy McBeath at Blairgowrie (1967). 'Arthur had a great love for his native music,' says Aly. 'Since his death, no one has been able to take his place. He was one of my true friends'

Aly's music back in the '60s: 'I had never heard a fiddle played like that before. I had never heard the clarity of tone or the volume or the beauty. I had never heard the *passion*.'

That phrase 'never heard before' cropped up a lot as I talked to people about their earliest recollections of Aly's impact. Apart from his technical skill – and it was always a natural, rather than mechanical, form of virtuosity – he brought to mainland Scotland a music that had only fleetingly been exposed outside of the Shetland isles, a perfectly formed mongrel music carrying Irish, American and even Scandinavian undertones and rhythms which made it sound strikingly different from the pedigree Scottish style.

More than that, though, he brought a very personal kind of magic, a way of playing which lifted everything his fiddle touched, whether it was a classic slow Perthshire air, an American country waltz or a wild improvisation on *The Mason's Apron*.

What is this thing called magic? It's evidently the same thing that bothered an old folky pal of mine many years ago as we listened to one of Aly's earliest Edinburgh sessions in the Buffs club: 'I don't know what the wee bugger's doing, but I wish somebody had taught me how to do it. Something just seems to happen.'

What happens, I think, is a sort of controlled emotional explosion. If I've learned one thing from all the time I've spent with him, it's that Aly Bain is a very emotional guy, deeply affected by the places, people, music and literature that he knows and loves, and, on the other side of the coin, easily moved to grief and anger by man's continuing inhumanity.

Generally, he keeps fairly tightlipped on all of this. That's why Cathal McConnell, one of his closest musical colleagues, is able to see him as 'a very private man'. It's when Aly plays that he lets a lot of it hang out.

I asked him once to name his favourite musician of all time. I confidently expected him to trot out one of the revered heroes from the pantheon of Scottish or Shetland fiddle music, perhaps James Scott Skinner, the north-east wizard, or Hector MacAndrew, whose stylish airs and strathspeys influenced Aly a great deal. But no. He thought for a while and then sprang the big surprise: Charlie Parker, the brilliant alto-sax player who changed the sound of jazz in the 1940s. Why Parker? 'For his heart and soul,' said Aly. 'When Parker recorded *Lover Man*, not long before he died, the emotion in his playing made his instrument sound the nearest to a human voice I've ever heard. It's so sad that I find it almost unbearable to listen to.'

Many people may have listened to Aly Bain playing some dark Celtic lament and gone through similar sensations.

So what we're looking at here is the stuff of which great music has always been made – the thrilling combustion that occurs when powerful emotions meet up with masterly musicianship.

There are, of course, many other elements that go into making Aly Bain the musician he is, and one of the purposes of this book is to identify those that are identifiable. Some of them are very obvious – for example, the early tuition he received from the late Tom Anderson, the Shetland guru whose dedication and determination were almost entirely responsible for the astonishing renaissance of fiddling in the islands. Today, thanks to Tom, the fiddle is taught in every Shetland school, and there are literally dozens of excellent young players. Tom was a strict, and occasionally pompous, adherent to what he perceived to be pure Shetland style, whereas the young Aly Bain had definite maverick tendencies. But the solid grounding that Tom gave Aly in bowing and fingering techniques was worth its weight in gold and was never forgotten. On another level, Tom taught Aly a lot about heritage and the significance of Shetland culture. In later years, while Tom didn't approve of everything his erstwhile pupil was getting up to on the international music scene, he was justifiably proud of Aly for spreading his beloved Shetland music all round the globe.

The globe-trotting began in 1970, when Aly made his first trip to the United States with the Scots guitarist Mike Whellans. Later, Bain and Whellans teamed up with the Northern Ireland duo of Robin Morton and Cathal McConnell under the

The deadly duo in the Halfway House, Edinburgh, when Aly and Mike were first interviewed by someone from The Scotsman *called Alastair Clark (1971)*

11

banner of the Boys of the Lough. The Boys made history. They were the first full-time professional group in Britain or Ireland playing only traditional music with an all-acoustic line-up. True, over in Dublin, the Chieftains had been making albums since the 1960s and had played in the States, but most of the Chieftains' members were still part-time musicians.

Fired by the dazzling front-line partnership of Bain's fiddle and McConnell's flute and whistle, the Boys quickly notched up a string of triumphs on British soil, notably the trendsetting Cambridge Folk Festival. But America beckoned: here was the biggest folk-music market in the world, and in terms of Celtic music it was almost entirely untapped. Touring with Mike Whellans, Aly had already made contact with agents and promoters who had witnessed the kind of impact that the young fiddler could have on American audiences. Robin Morton, who had taken on the task of looking after the Boys' affairs as well as doing the musical business on concertina and bodhran, began doing the liaison work for a tour that would whisk the Boys through some of the best coffee-house joints on the east coast, as well as two of the biggest festivals, Fox Hollow and Philadelphia.

It was a bold, pioneering decision – the United States folk scene, like its counterpart in Britain, was still singers' territory, and the instrumental music that did exist was overwhelmingly American. But that first tour, in 1972, opened many ears and opened many doors. It was not only an important springboard for the Boys of the Lough – since then, they have toured the US no fewer than forty-two times, leaving their Edinburgh base to spend several months there every year – but it also blazed a trail for numerous other instrumental bands to follow from both Scotland and Ireland. There have been tours, too, in Australia, India, Japan and all over Europe.

Aly Bain is still with the Boys. Next to his two daughters, Annalese and Jessica, they are, he says, 'the love of my life', and he is the first to admit that without the stability and stimulation that the band provides he might never have had the courage to take on other solo challenges – he is much in demand for guest appearances at Scotland's biggest open-air rock events, has had a fiddle 'shoot-out' on stage with Stephane Grappelli, has played on recordings by such disparate stars as Richard Thompson and Fish, and, at the 1992 Edinburgh International Festival, mounted a two-man show with the poet Norman MacCaig.

The long friendship with MacCaig goes back to the early 1970s, when Aly was staying at the Edinburgh home of Dolina Maclennan, the Gaelic singer and actress, and her husband, George Brown. Doli's house in Thirlestane Road always seemed to have a poet or some wandering minstrel in it in those days. The first meeting between the lanky, craggy-featured MacCaig and the Shetland fiddler did not augur well. They had a stern argument about the role of emotion in art, with Norman, in typically caustic style, claiming that as soon as he felt that a poem was becoming emotional he threw it into the dustbin, and Aly berating him for what he saw as an act of cultural folly. But the two men went on to become the closest of friends, bound together by a great mutual respect.

Words and music: with Norman MacCaig for The Pen and the Fiddle *shows at the Traverse Theatre, Edinburgh (1992)*

The show with MacCaig at the Traverse Theatre was built on the delightfully simple foundation of a few tunes, some conversation, and poems. In a way, it was a natural progression from some of the work that Aly had been doing on television. His TV career really took off in 1984, when Aly got together with producer Mike Alexander and writer Douglas Eadie to prepare a series that was to become an innovative classic.

Down Home, which took viewers on a fascinating trek along the long and winding trail of fiddle music that led across the Atlantic and through the United States and Canada, was not simply the first film to examine the links between North American and Scottish music. More important, it was a deliberate, and highly successful, attempt to break away from standard documentary tactics. It allowed the music and

Aly joins writer Alastair Clark and manager Liz Wright for an impromptu traditional dance in the Whirlie office in Edinburgh to celebrate the completion of another paragraph

the musicians to speak for themselves, with a musician, Aly, acting not as 'presenter' but as participant.

More Aly Bain television films followed, notably one on Cajun music, and, most recently, a major series on the Shetland Folk Festival.

With the television has come, inevitably, fame among the general public. Billy Connolly points from his hotel window in Glasgow and says: 'Ask the people out there in the streets how many fiddlers they know. His name's first on the lips every time. That's an amazing achievement.'

It's important to remember that this kind of recognition has been achieved without a single artistic compromise on Aly's part. He has never attempted to be anything other than himself on television, playing the traditional music he wants to play in the way he loves to play it. No kilts. No wiggles. No winks. No false bonhomie. No stuffed-dummy smile. No extravagant sweeps of the bow. No musical rubbish. No cheap thrills. What you get on the small screen is what you get on stage: Aly Bain straight, no chaser. So when he is greeted by strangers, as he is wherever he goes in Scotland – in the street, in the supermarket, in the pub – they feel they know him well enough to approach him as they would approach a pal: 'Hi, Aly. How're you dae'n these days?'

Right now, he's dae'n just fine, thank you very much. He lives in Edinburgh in a part of Stockbridge known as the Colonies – rows of neat little houses that jut in toothcomb rows from the south bank of the Water of Leith river. Construction of the Colonies was begun in 1861 by the Edinburgh Co-operative Building Society, to provide low-priced homes for working people. Nowadays they tend to be snapped up by the 'yuppie' brigade, but Aly, a left-winger all his life, is proud to be living in a place that has such robust working-class roots.

Aly's house, like the others, has a tiny front garden in which you could just about swing a golf club if you were that desperate. Literally a stone's throw away is Glenogle Baths, where Aly can be found most mornings of the week, methodically swimming his thirty lengths.

Inside the house, he has put his joinery skills to good use, transforming a basic living space into a cosy des. res., with faultless pinewood workmanship to be found round every corner. The sitting-room, which appears to double as music room, is noticeably lacking in sitting furniture. There is a solitary couch upon which Aly and any visitors have to be accommodated. It also serves as a convenient and convivial overnight 'crash' for pals who haven't managed to last the frenetic pace of a heavy evening at Aly's favourite local pub, the Bailie Bar. The walls of the room carry several framed photographs of mean-looking seagulls – a bizarre touch, perhaps, amid a

Family trio: Aly's daughters, Jessica (left) and Annalese, are his pride and joy

collection that includes pictures of Aly with musician friends from the States and Shetland and pictures of his children, through the growing ages. There is, too, Norman MacCaig's handwritten poem, *Shetland Reel*, dedicated to Aly.

Within walking distance from the house is the office which Aly set up a few years ago when his solo career started to snowball. It's run by Liz Wright, who, in Aly's words, 'really has organised my life and made me a better human being'. Liz's previous experience had been organising the lives of the rock group Simple Minds, and for a while she also handled the affairs of the Scots television star Muriel Gray. Aly's solo operations have expanded to such an extent that he has now become a full-time job — one that Liz tackles with great, infectious gusto.

Aly lives on his own. He and his American wife, Lucy, are still great friends, but they got divorced in 1991 after a marriage which began promisingly enough with not one wedding ceremony but two. First of all came the American wedding, held in Ardsley, New York State. Then, with television cameras recording every step, smile and fiddle tune, the couple went through a traditional country-style wedding ritual in Shetland.

Lucy lives in another part of Edinburgh with Annalese and Jessica, now in their mid-teens, who are frequent visitors to The Colonies when Aly is off the road and relaxing.

'I belong to Shetland, but Edinburgh is really my home, and has been for the past twenty years,' says Aly. 'It's a beautiful city and not too big — a good place to raise children. I love the oldness and history of the city. It gives me a feeling of continuity and permanence. I love the sense of culture — there is so much happening every year, with the Edinburgh Festival and so on. Most of my friends live here. I love the pubs and the atmosphere of the place. I've been in so many beautiful places around the world, but I don't think I could live anywhere else than Edinburgh. By living here, I keep in touch with what is most important to me — a sense of being Scots.'

At the same time, Shetland is never far from his thoughts, and certainly never far from his music. The writer Douglas Sutherland suggested to me that Aly's fiddling is 'all about aching for the islands', and when I put this to the fiddler himself he nodded his head and said: 'Douglas could have a point there.'

Aly still makes frequent trips to Shetland, which lies so far north of the Scottish mainland that many atlases conveniently re-position it in a separate box somewhere in a spare expanse of North Sea. While constantly bemoaning the punitive cost of the return flight — he can get from Edinburgh to Boston and back for the same money — Aly is unable to resist the tug of the isles where he lived his childhood and teens.

On a recent visit to the Shetland Folk Festival, I was alarmed to see him wandering across the busy street that runs by Lerwick harbour, seemingly oblivious of the grunting lorries and snarling cars that had to take evasive action in order to keep fiddle music alive. He made it, unscathed, to the other side and said: 'I wish I could remember that there's *traffic* in Shetland these days.'

The traffic springs largely from oil, which was discovered in the seas off the islands in the 1960s and which has transformed not only the streets of Lerwick but also the lives of many Shetlanders. Before the oil, the main pillars of Shetland's economy had been fish and sheep. The fish trade is still actually the islands' biggest employer, even if the boom times are over. But the building of Europe's biggest oil and gas terminal at Sullom Voe, on the northern tip of the Shetland mainland, and the subsequent growth of permanent employment, coupled with the injection of massive oil revenues, has enabled Shetland not only to escape the worst of the worldwide economic recession but also to tuck away millions of pounds for that rainy day when Sullom Voe's vast storage tanks lie empty and rusting.

So the Shetland that Aly Bain describes in the following pages is not the Shetland that you will find easily today unless you go rooting around some of the smaller, more remote isles. One of his reasons for setting down his recollections on paper was to describe a way of life that had existed virtually unchanged since the arrival of the motor car, but which has all but disappeared in a dramatically short space of time.

Aly's literary opus, neatly handwritten in ruled exercise books, was actually begun as a projected autobiography. Over a period of many months, he stuck to the task manfully, in spite of burgeoning concert and television commitments, but it finally became painfully evident to the publisher and to Aly himself that at this rate of progress the book would take years to complete. As it happened, Aly had reached a kind of natural break, taking his story more or less up to the point where he was about to leave Shetland for Glasgow at the age of twenty-two.

Aly's description of his Shetland upbringing is such a loving and sensitive one, and so lucidly expressed, that it was immediately clear to me that his written words should form a complete section of this book, without a lot of pernickety editorial meddling by me or anybody else. (Incidentally, just in case you're wondering, I have nowhere in this book put words into Aly Bain's mouth: he and I both despise the increasingly prevalent practice of 'ghost-writing', and the only spirit that appeared from time to time in our collaboration did so in the cheering form of the finest cooking whisky in the world, Black Bottle.)

What follows in the next chapter, then, is Aly's solo, his story of his Shetland.

Aly's grandfather Magnus, left, with his brothers Malcolm and John. The caps reveal the influence of the Dutch fishermen who sailed to Shetland waters for the herring

Chapter Two

THE FIDDLER'S TALE

PART I   DOWN HOME, SHETLAND

I first opened my eyes in my parents' bed at 19 Market Street on 15 May 1946 – the result, I am sure, of a welcome-home-from-war embrace! My mother and father hadn't seen each other for two or more years while he served with the Royal Navy in Iceland, and no doubt they made up for lost time. This must have been happening all over Shetland, because ours was easily the biggest class at school.

There I was in Lerwick, beautiful Lerwick, stone-grey on the outside but warm on the inside; the place where my feet would stomp around for the next twenty-one years. How lucky I was to be born in that lovely town, its harbour a refuge for fishermen and seamen since the days of the Norsemen and before. After more than twenty years of travelling around the world, I still believe that Shetland is the most beautiful place that I have ever experienced: the islands surrounded by cliffs and sea, everything so clean; the air, the sky, the hills, the lochs and the burns. It was a wonderland in which to grow up and explore.

My mother and father were both from Sandwick, on the southern part of the Shetland mainland. My father, Laurence Malcomson Bain, came from a croft at Cullister Köll. 'Köll' is the Norse derivation meaning rounded-top hill, while 'bister' means farm or settlement. My mother, Jemima Tulloch Smith, came from the Whirlie Croft, about a mile away from Cullister. I don't know the exact meaning of 'whirlie', but there are a few of them in Shetland and they are all crofts where the house stands near a burn. I was told that the name came from a whirlie pool (swirling pool).

My father had five brothers and three sisters. He always talked of his childhood being happy but hard; like most people, they had very little money. As soon as he was old enough, he had to pull his weight and turn his hand to any crofting work. For a man with a burning desire to be educated, he was in the wrong place at the wrong time. He left school after a basic education and started serving his time as a cooper, nearby at Broonistaing.

Aly's father with his cooper pals during the late 1930s

Mother and father in pre-Aly days, probably 1939

Aly's father, Laurence ('Lol'), a proud and wonderful craftsman, in his workshop with his beloved tools

Aly's great-grandparents with his grandmother
at the Whirlie croft (1908)

Aly's grandfather, Andrew, at twenty-four,
before emigrating to America, where he worked in
the tin mines of Colorado

People talk about the craftsmanship of great musicians, writers and painters. Well, my father was a fine and skilled cooper. Watching him making a herring barrel was like seeing a work of art appear before one's eyes. He would make nine full-sized barrels every day. This was no mean feat, and I loved watching him making so many, shaping the staves and, best of all, driving down the hoops, swinging his two-pound hammer like a feather. He would be stripped to the waist, shining with sweat, his body rippling with muscles. My mother told me how she loved his physique, and I used to look at my dad as he got older and wonder how any human frame could take such a hammering and survive.

Before the war, he moved to Lerwick to work his trade. At this time, the herring industry was in full swing, with hundreds of boats bringing in thousands of crans of fish every day. By then, he was engaged to my mother, who disliked the name Jemima and was always known as Minnie. She had two sisters and one brother.

I was a frequent visitor to the Whirlie, and remember it from my earliest days. The way of life had remained very much the same for hundreds of years: no electricity, just the shadowy light of the Tilley lamps. The croft had no luxuries, but was warm and cosy.

As a girl, my mother found school a welcome escape from life on the croft. Like my father, she saw education as her way out. Unfortunately, because she was a woman,

Aly's father's family, in their Sunday best. Back (left to right): John, William, Magnus, Peter, Laurence (Aly's father). Front: Celia, grandfather Magnus, Babs, Bertie, grandmother Mary and Marian. The picture was taken during the late 1930s, and Celia, Bertie and Magnus are the only survivors

this was never to be. My grandfather thought that she would be more use on the croft, and that was that. This had a lasting effect on the way my mother thought, and she became a feminist and, in later life, a radical socialist, defending the Soviet Union and Lenin to the hilt. Who could blame her for her hardline attitude to politics? Opportunities just weren't available to her generation, especially women.

Her father, Andrew, was a hard-working man with little time for fun. He was small, strong and very handsome. He was known for his wild temper and was called Herod by the locals, after the biblical king. Having gone to America and worked at the tin mines in Colorado, he returned home to marry my grandmother and build the Whirlie Croft. His wife, Martha Smith, was kind and gentle: I remember her well because she stayed in Lerwick with us for a few years before she died.

My brother Douglas was born in 1939, just before the war. He was followed two years later by my sister Audrey, but she died from a severe attack of measles when she was only two years old. Her death shattered my parents, and I don't think they ever got over it. When my dad died in 1988, we found her little shoes hanging in the window of his garden shed. Even after forty years, the mentioning of her name would bring tears to my parents' eyes.

I remember little of my life at Market Street, but it was undoubtedly where I had my first introduction to fiddle music. Our neighbours were Tom Anderson and his wife, Babs. Like my father, Tom was not long back from the war, and had resumed his passion for playing the fiddle. He told me later that when he practised, I used to crawl across the landing to listen. Then he would sit me on his knee and play for me. Indeed, my first memory of the fiddle is of the scroll hanging down over my head. I can't have been more than eighteen months old at the time. It was also then that I met the great guitarist Willie Johnson, who came to rehearse with Tom. I didn't know at the time, of course, how important a part these two men would play in my later life and how they would become two of my dearest friends.

Our flat in Market Street was very small for the four of us. We moved from there when I was two, and I remember sitting in the front of the lorry with my mother, heading for our luxury council house, with its own garden, at 19 Russell Crescent.

Our new street was like a building site, with houses going up everywhere. By the time it was finished, there were thirty or forty young families living around us in this, the newest part of Lerwick. A few hundred yards to the south was the Clickimin Loch with its big pictish broch where we used to play, not cowboys and Indians but Vikings and Picts (I wonder how many children have ever played this on a real pictish fort?). To the east lay the sea, only a short distance from the house, where we played among the rocks and small cliffs from dawn until dusk.

Tom Anderson with a handsome young Willie Johnson in the early 1950s

*Aly at two years old, just after the family had
moved to Russell Crescent. The new council house was
in the middle of a building site*

Life was one big adventure, with none of today's dangers. Few cars. Just the freedom to roam wherever we chose. We lived in and out of each other's houses; doors were never locked, and crime was something we had never even heard of.

Only two things stood between me and complete happiness as a child – school and peats! I hated school only marginally more than helping my father with his exploits on the peat hill. Peat was, of course, our main source of domestic fuel, but even the prospect of warm winter nights did nothing to heighten its appeal to me. Early in the month of May every year, my father's eyes would take on a new light, and when the first fine weather arrived this look would change to one of glee. He would fetch his tushkar (peat-cutting spade) and head for the hill. There, he would cut as many as three hundred bags of peat.

Again, this was hard work, but it brought out the artist in him and he cut his peats perfectly. The peat hill was about a mile along the north road from Lerwick, and it seemed as if every able man from the town was up there cutting. There was even a bus service to ferry them to and from the hill. Among other things, the peat-cutting was a social act. The men would discuss the qualities of the peat and compare tushkars, meanwhile working like hell. Once the peats were cut, they were laid out to dry until a skin formed on them, making them easy to handle. After a few weeks, depending on the weather, the next stage would be to raise them. This was where we came in. My brother Douglas, who was six years older than me and already an expert, actually enjoyed this, and my father would drag me with my mother and him to raise the peat. The idea was to lay one peat on its side and to balance three or four more on their ends against it, so that the wind (never absent in Shetland!) would whistle through and dry them. After a couple of weeks, bigger raisings would be made. Not content with that, we then had to 'roog' the peats – making them into small stacks, surrounding the dry peats with the heavier mossy ones to protect them from the rain. All this was done with an aching back and eyes full of peat dust. When the time came to put them in bags and barrow them down to the road, it was enough to finish me off. The arrival of the peats at home was a big occasion. All the neighbours would help to carry them to our back green, where my father would carefully stow them in his peatshed.

The end of the peat season meant for me the end of four months of misery. When I was older, around fourteen, my father actually made me a tushkar and presented it to me with a look of undying hope in his eyes, like a laird presenting his son with his first Purdy shotgun. I trudged after him to the hill with the enthusiasm of a victim bound for the firing squad. However, luck was with me. As I cut my first peat, the tushkar snapped. I wish a photographer could have been there to catch the look of sadness in my father's face and the look of joy on mine.

Like most people, I will never forget my first day at school, the old infant school in Lerwick. Unwilling to leave the safety of my mother's side or let go of her hand, I walked into the classroom, with its oak desks, and sat down expecting to be done some terrible harm.

For a while, everything was fine and the teachers were kind and patient. One memory that sticks in my mind was the percussion band, where we all stood around banging various instruments – castanets, triangles and out-of-tune drums. I think this put me off percussion for life. I also used to sing a little song called *Peter Yell*, which I've never forgotten. I was sent to the headmistress for some misdemeanor. I stood outside her door, shaking in my shoes, but all she made me do was sing *Peter Yell* while she and some other teachers fell about laughing. It went like this, in a Shetland dialect to the tune of *The Lovat Scouts*:

> Peter Yell is a funny peerie man,
> His een is a' geen squint,
> His neck sticks oot lik a clokin duke
> And he beckons doon behint.

My first folk song!

Primary school was fine, except that for some reason I soon began to resist education. I felt closed in at school, and we had an odd teacher who didn't seem to like children – there seems to be one at every school. I suppose I was nervous and quite lacking in confidence. I don't think that I wasn't bright; something just went wrong. I

JUNE
1953

Central Public School, Lerwick
1953

ALISTER
Bain

The class of '53. Aly is first left, front row

began to dislike school, and slowly it became like a prison. I would sit there and not hear anything. I wanted to fly out of the window, to be free.

I failed my 11-plus exam. The thought that my education was put on trial at such an early age has always appalled me. When we went on to secondary school there were three categories: M for Modified, T for Technical and C for Commercial. Nowadays it seems like something from Charles Dickens. I was in the T's and decided to take Navigation, not really because I wanted to go to sea but because it meant that we were allowed to sail around the harbour. Our teacher, Tommy Moncrieff, had an old sixern, and we learned to row and sail outside in the fresh air – which was where I wanted to be. However, I soon came to realise that the sea was not for me, and so with a few pals decided to boldly go where no man had gone before: we took up cookery! We all loved it and became quite good at it (which was just as well, as we had to eat what we had made). The only prize I ever won at school was third place for my steak and kidney pie, which must have been good as the teacher ate it all.

The other thing I enjoyed about school was our band. The teachers discovered that some of us could play and encouraged us to get together for school concerts. There was fiddle, mandolin, drums, guitar, piano and bass. The music was mainly skiffle, with some country-and-western and, of course, our own reels and jigs. Fortunately, our rehearsals coincided with the subjects I didn't like – algebra and geometry. The band was called the Rhythm Aces. We were good and often played at local concerts. The bass player, Ron Mathieson, was the only other member of that band to make a career in music. Even at that age, he was an incredibly talented pianist and bassist. His first

The school band, The Rhythm Aces (left to right): Sonny Morrison, Wilma Robertson, John Tulloch, Aly, Ronnie Mathieson

love in music was jazz, and in later years he went on to become one of the leading jazz bass players in Europe, appearing with many of the top international names. In our band, though, he wasn't allowed a real bass – instead, he played an old tea-chest with a string and pole.

School would have been fun if it had been confined to music, history and art. But it wasn't, of course, and for me the maths and science were a nightmare. I made up my mind to leave as soon as possible, and that's what I did in 1961 at the age of fifteen.

If my feelings for school were apprehensive, life at home was content and wonderful. My parents were happy in their new house, and in 1951, when I was six, along came my sister Anne. They had longed for a little girl after the death of Audrey, and Anne fulfilled all their hopes, making our family complete at last.

Anne was born in the new maternity wing of the hospital, and I can remember looking out of the window to see my mother carry her new baby through the gate. My mother's sister, Aunt Betty, who had been looking after us, said: 'Here's your new sister.' I asked where she had come from, and she told me that a stork had taken her to the hospital. I was confused, to say the least, as we didn't have storks in Shetland. If she had told me that it was a black-backed gull I might have believed her.

Around this age, I started to go to stay with my relations on my own at weekends. At first, I spent most time at the Whirlie, my mother's croft. The life of my mother's brother, Andy, consisted of horses, ploughs, hens, sheep, fencing and peat-cutting. It was a life of endless toil. There was no such thing as a holiday or time off. Andy and his wife Nessie worked the croft and lived there with their two sons, Michael and Russell, who were roughly the same age as me. My mother would put me on the bus at Lerwick for the fifteen-mile journey to Sandwick. The bus was always full of smoke, and inevitably I would feel sick. So there I would sit with my little case and my dried-milk tin to be sick in. All this would soon be forgotten and my ever-brewing nausea would be washed away by the excitement of arriving.

I loved the countryside. My granny, Martha, who was still living at the croft, took me to the burn and taught me how to fish for trout. I've been a keen fisherman ever since. The equipment in those days was not very sophisticated: a primitive rod, consisting of a bamboo cane, a line, a cork, and a bent pin. All we needed then was a tin full of juicy worms, and off we'd go. There are no rivers in Shetland, but some of the burns are quite big. The Whirlie burn belonged to the smaller variety, and in some places it was almost completely grown over. Still, it was full of little trout, six to eight inches long, and when we had caught enough for a meal we would take them home and coat them in flour and fry them in butter. What a sweet, wild flavour they had, especially with our fresh-air appetites. In the mornings, I loved looking for the hens' eggs; they were often still warm and we would rush home to fry them with bacon for breakfast. The so-called free-range eggs sold in supermarkets today have only one thing in common with the Whirlie eggs: they're the same shape.

In those days, all the ploughing was done by horses, and my uncle had a chestnut Icelandic pony called Nelly, who had a lovely temperament. We used to ride her

Survivors of the 1950s: a family reunion in Lerwick, where Aly's Elvis hairstyle was all the rage

bareback and in the winter hitch her to a sledge, hanging on with our freezing hands as she pulled us behind her through the snow.

There were two neighbours not far from the Whirlie in a croft called Veister. Sydie and Martha lived in an older-style but 'n' ben with a thatched roof. Martha wore a moorit (brown wool) Shetland hap (wrap) around her head and shoulders and Sydie had a grand moustache and smoked a pipe. His favourite tobacco was black twist, and when funds were low it would be tea-leaves or peat that filled his pipe. They had an old American stove for heat, with four lids on top. One of them was always left open so that Sydie could spit down into the fire. He was an expert at spitting, and no matter where he was in the room the spit would fly through the air and claim a direct hit every time.

When you wanted to go in and see the old couple you had to sneak past Mossy, the biggest, worst-tempered sheepdog I ever met. She would sit taking up most of the passage, and depending on whether she knew you she would lean over and let you pass, or you'd lose at least a trouser leg. The postman lived in terror of Mossy. Eventually, he got fed up and just threw the mail over the fence.

Inside the house was always full of herring nets dangling from the ceiling waiting to be mended. The croft was always dark inside because of its tiny window – it had been built to keep the weather out rather than let the light in – so the nets would be repaired against a white sheet.

Like so many Shetlanders in those days, Sydie and Martha had nothing to give but kindness, and they were never short of it. Sydie rolled me my first cigarette, which was a bit of mossy peat rolled up in newspaper. I tried to pretend to enjoy it like a grown-up, while coughing and spluttering at the taste in my mouth. Sydie loved telling stories of local characters and his younger days – sadly, I can't remember any of those tales now. They had a wonderful old battery wireless set, and at one o'clock every day Sydie would wander over and tune in for the news. A faint voice, accompanied by various whistles and whines, would announce the BBC, and then usually the battery would die. I always ran down to Veister to say cheerio to Sydie and Martha on a Sunday night before taking the bus back to Lerwick. They always had something for me, sometimes a sweetie, but more often a puffed-wheat box full of fresh eggs, each one wrapped in paper. To me, it was worth a million pounds.

The days at Whirlie were a rich part of my childhood, and I'll never forget them. Uncle Andy worked so hard that I hardly ever saw him on my visits. He was always doing something round the croft, and when he'd finished he would come home and knit on the machine until late. As all-rounders, crofters could not be beaten: they could turn their hands to anything. Their knowledge of working both land and sea is a testament to human survival. There was also an equality between men and women – they shared the work between them and worked as hard as each other. In many cases, when the menfolk were at the fishing for long periods, the women would have to tend to all the tasks around the croft as well as raise the children.

When I was around ten or eleven, I started to visit my father's sister, Aunt Celia, in Hoswick. Hoswick could almost be described as a town, with fifty or so houses built on a hillside next to the sea at Sandwick. There were plenty of children of my own age to play with – in fact, I was related to most of them in one way or another. My father had another sister and three brothers living in and around Hoswick, so I was never short of aunts, uncles and cousins to visit. Fishing was my favourite pastime, and my equally fanatical pal, Geordie Munro, and I used to walk two miles up to the dam at Channerwick burn and fish it all the way down to the sea. We often caught as many as thirty little brown trout in a day. There was a deep pool near the sea, known as the Queenie Hole, where, at the end of August, if we were lucky we caught beautiful silvery sea trout.

At night, we would get up to all sorts of mischief, especially at Hallowe'en. One of our tricks was to pull up turnips and then knock on some poor unfortunate's door. When the door was opened, in would go the turnips, and we'd all run for our lives. Another version was to find a house with easy access to the roof. The idea was for one of us to sneak up quickly and deposit a square of peat over the chimney, then retire to a safe distance. After a few minutes, the sounds of coughing would be followed by the sight of the inhabitants bursting through their front door, followed by bellows of smoke. Fortunately, in those days there was nothing much which could be ruined in the houses.

These mean tricks were saved only for Hallowe'en, and for the rest of the year the population lived in comparative safety. My aunt was very kind, especially as she had to

Up-Helly Aa, around 1959. Back row (left to right): Willie Hutchison, Joe Hunter, Douglas Thompson, Frankie Black, Bertie Simpson, Billy Moncrieff. Front: Arthur Laurenson, Alex Greig, Aly, Alison Bain

put up with a great deal. I recall that she had luxuries in the house which we could never afford, like orange squash. The best thing they had was the radiogram, which could play one '78' after another. I used to go to bed with ten Harry Lauder records lined up to play. I was soon asleep, and my aunt told me later how, when she folded my clothes, she found little trout hidden in all my pockets. Her husband, Jack Nicholson, was a sea captain and often away, so I think she enjoyed having me visit.

I had started playing the fiddle when I was eleven and, as luck would have it, just a few doors away from my aunt lived one of Shetland's most renowned fiddlers, Bob Duncan. He was a truly great player, and had a band with the rest of his family. They would play at local dances – indeed, they played at my parents' wedding. Bob was also a cooper, and my father served his apprenticeship under him at Broonistaing. I used to go along to his house to listen to him playing the fiddle. He loved James Scott Skinner and had a collection of his records, which he kept in mint condition. Bob could play every Skinner tune, even the most complicated pieces, without a flaw. He was a slow sort of person, not prone to sudden movements, but when he played the fiddle he came to life. He played the slow airs with his eyes closed, swaying on his feet, lost in the melody as if he were asleep. One of the best pieces of advice ever given to me came from Willie Johnson, the guitarist, who said that the first thing you have to do when learning music is to learn to listen. There were many gifted players among the older generation, and I was fortunate enough to hear and see most of them play.

My father was still working as a cooper in Lerwick, and in the summer holidays he used to take me on the crossbar of his bicycle out to the fish-curing station. During the winter and spring months, he would make anything up to two thousand barrels – nine full-size or thirteen half barrels each day. There must have been around a dozen curing stations in Lerwick at the time. My father worked for Alexander Wood & Sons, who were based in Fraserburgh. At the landing season – June, July and August – all of the barrels were filled with salt herring. Each station had a wooden pier, where the boats would land their catch, and I knew every boat by its number. They had lovely names like the *Ocean Reaper*, the *Research*, the *Dauntless*, the *Morning Star*, the *Snowdrop* and the *Serene*. The curing yard was frantic with activity from early morning until late at night. The gutters' fingers would fairly fly; in one quick move the herring were gutted and thrown to the packers, who would lay them belly up in the barrels and cover each layer with salt. All of the gutters and packers were women; some of them were native Shetlanders, but most were from Fraserburgh, Peterhead and other ports in north-east Scotland, with some from as far away as Donegal in Ireland.

It was the perfect place for a small boy to get in a mess. I would come home stinking of fish, with my hair full of scales. In order to keep me out of the way, my father would tie me to the end of the pier, from where I could fish for piltocks. I would sit with my feet dangling over the edge and lower scraps of herring on a line to where I could see them swimming. Some of the piltock and young saithe were bigger than me and when I caught one I had to shout for help to pull it up.

For me, every day was an adventure. I became friendly with many of the workers, and for the first time in my life I heard dialects from other places and listened to them in amazement. The workers from the north-east used to call me Lol Bain's Loon as I sat happily fishing at the end of the pier. Catching the piltocks was easy and there was always fun to be had, but a new challenge appeared one day in the shape of a conger eel. It can't have been more than a few feet long, but it was certainly longer than I was and from where I stood it looked like a python. I had heard stories of how congers could bite your hand off, and that even when their heads were cut off they could grow another, even bigger than the last! While I was desperate to catch the eel, I was dreading the prospect of actually doing so. He lived right at the bottom on the sand, and the main problem was to get my bait down to him without the other fish getting it first. My only chance was with a heavy sinker. I dropped my bait in and, to my horror, the eel swam around it a few times and then, in one huge gulp, swallowed the lot. With my heart in my mouth, I pulled for all I was worth. With both feet against the end of the pier, I heaved for what seemed an eternity until the head of this thing rose out of the water, more terrifying than anything you could see in a horror film. One more heave and it arrived on the pier. I was in total panic by now, as the eel thrashed around my feet – I expected one of them to be bitten off at any minute. I untied myself from the pier and fled to a safe distance. The eel lay there for a while. Various people came to look at it, but I never went near the poor thing. I never tried to catch another conger eel: piltocks were safer.

The herring industry was well into decline at this point, although it was still a major annual event in Shetland's calendar. Hundreds of workers would arrive for the short landing season and inject new life into Lerwick. They all lived in what were called simply the Huts – a row of low-slung black wooden huts built just above each curing station. They had bunk beds, sleeping as many as four or six to one room. The Huts were all inhabited by young women, who, of course, excited much interest in many of the local young men. Stories of wild parties, frantic fiddle music and dancing (among other things) would be reported through the town every week. I can remember the unenviable task of the apprentice cooper whose job was to get them up in the morning at five or six. One year, my dad's apprentice was sent off to wake everyone for work. Without knowing the dangerous nature of his assignment, he banged on the first door without any apprehension. The response was sudden: the door opened and he went in, only to reappear a few moments later, stripped of his clothes, barely clinging to his underpants, and followed by a bucket of cold water and the sound of screeching laughter from within. These women were entitled to their fun, for they worked long, hard hours for very little pay. There was always a sense of competition in their work, as the packers would have to keep up with the gutters, who could work incredibly fast. Not only did they gut the herring but they also selected the quality of them at the same time, throwing them over their shoulders into the appropriate basket without so much as a glance.

Sometimes tempers would get frayed, and the coopers were called in to calm things down. There was no let-up until all herrings were packed away and the yard and oilskins hosed down. If there were big shots of herring landed, the work continued through until dawn and then everyone would drag themselves off to bed, exhausted, too tired for fun.

My father had a great deal of respect for the women. In spite of all the hard work, cracked skin and cut fingers stinging with salt, their humour always came through. They found time to be kind to me, too, and I have happy memories of those days.

However, my father's days as a cooper were numbered. He practically ran the yard – hiring the workers, buying the herring and doing the accounts. He asked for a small pay rise for the extra work he was doing, and the company refused. They didn't expect him to leave, but for him it was a matter of principle, so he packed his tools. His boss came to our house for two or three nights in a row trying to persuade him back with more money than he had originally asked for. But his mind was made up, and nothing could change it.

In any case, the days of exported salt herring were virtually over and the only remaining buyers, the Soviet Union and Spain, had built their own fishing fleets. A few years after my father left, the coopers, gutters and packers disappeared, as did the greatest industry Shetland has ever known. Around the turn of the century, almost a million barrels of salt herring were exported in one season from the islands. Oil now brings more money, but the herring fishing employed thousands of people. It changed our culture and brought new blood on to the islands. Lerwick became known as Scottie Toon and new strains of fiddle music echoed around its streets. Buskers appeared, like blind George Stark from Dundee, who brought strathspeys, marches and the music of

George Stark ('The Blind Fiddler'), from Dundee, with Willie Jordan. George first visited Shetland in 1902 to busk during the herring season, and continued to do so every year until 1959, with the exception of the war years. He died in 1960, aged 83. He was once playing The Bonnie Lass of Bon Accord *in Union Street, Aberdeen, when he felt a tap on his shoulder and a voice saying, 'Can ye no' play it right?'*
'My Goad,' said George, 'it was Scott Skinner himself!'

Scott Skinner. The Irish workers brought their music, too, leaving a rich legacy which remains to this day.

Life at home remained unchanged. Dad found a job in the hospital laundry, which he kept for a couple of years before becoming a handyman for the Shetland (or Zetland, as it was called then) County Council architects department. At least he was back working with wood again. We also got a knitting machine to provide extra income. I can still hear the sound of it in my ears – 'zip, zip, zip', all night long. Dad would work the machine, which was a big, heavy affair, and my mother would finish off the jumpers, sewing on the necks and sleeves.

Rarely was there ever a peaceful night in front of the fire. It was always work, work, work for them. But the extra income was invaluable, and with it we could afford a few luxuries. Out went the old linoleum, to be replaced by carpets, and – most important as far as I was concerned – we acquired an HMV radiogram. I remember it being carried into the corner of the sitting-room, the latest piece of technology, shining and new, in our house. My dad's taste in music was bang up to date: Ruby Murray and Michael Halliday singing *Magic Moments*.

The most boring day of the week was Sunday. During the 1950s, there was a strange religious hangover from earlier times. Even though neither of my parents could possibly be described as 'kirky' folk, we were nevertheless sent to Sunday school. I knew that my parents did not believe in God, but all the other children went, so we had to go. After dreading school all week, I was never too happy about attending another one on Sunday – what a nerve. We were groomed and clothed in our Sunday best. My hair was flattened over to one side. I wore a newly ironed shirt, short trousers and finally ankle socks and Clarks sandals. We were so perfect that we were frightened to lean on anything. The first job was to fetch the milk from Billy Bain's dairy. To walk all the way there and back without kicking a stone or climbing a wall required enormous will-power! Then, boring beyond belief, was Sunday school itself – a crowd of small children, fidgeting and restless, all dying to be outside. All those figures on stained-glass windows staring down at us while we heard the story of the Good Samaritan for the hundredth time. You would think that he was the only one who had ever done someone a good turn.

Even at that age, try as I would, I just couldn't believe in God any more than I could believe in Thor or Odin. I respect people's right to worship whatever they want, but to me as a child the Church of Scotland was hardly an enjoyable place, except when it was time for the Sunday School picnic or the Christmas party. The only thing we were allowed to do on a Sunday was to go for a walk with our parents. There was no playing of any kind allowed; it was a day for being seen and not heard. Often, my brother and I would sneak downstairs after my parents had gone to bed and listen to the Top Twenty on Radio Luxembourg. We would have the sound so low that our ears were pressed against the speaker.

It was mainly my father who was strict regarding our behaviour on Sundays. He had come from a church-going family, and, being sentimental about his childhood, he was, I think, reluctant to change the old ways. Even though he was a non-believer, his favourite programme was *Songs of Praise*. He truly loved the old hymns, and I can see him yet listening to his favourite, *By Cool Salom*, with tears rolling down his cheeks. I understand how he felt, because when I hear those hymns now I think of him and I have to fight back my own tears. My mother, on the other hand, had no time at all for religion. Her family wasn't religious in any real way, and she considered the whole thing to be a plot by the Establishment to subdue the people. There were real memories in her generation of how the Church sided with the landowners against the people in the time of their grandparents.

My mother was a kind, gentle woman who hardly raised her voice, but she despised injustice of any kind. The subject of religion wasn't a big issue in our house, unlike some others. In fact, it was hardly ever discussed at all, as we all agreed about it. The subject of Sunday school, however, initiated my first challenge against their authority. I fought them tooth and nail every Sunday, standing nearer to my mother, as I knew she didn't really care anyway. In the end, my father gave up, and before long we were even fishing and playing football on Sundays.

During the 1950s, people's attitudes were strange to say the least. I remember those post-war years as movies full of people called Ginger, Chalky and Sandy fighting wars; the ever-virginal Doris Day; endless teenagers, the boys in shorts with hairy legs and the females bursting into womanhood dressed to look like little girls. Only Little Richard and Elvis saved us – and, of course, Fats Domino too.

The Shetland winter begins for me the first of September. There is not really an autumn. One day the weather changes, and suddenly it's winter. September and October bring heavy rain and gales; soon the sea trout shoot up the burns to the hill lochs and spawn in the little burns that feed them. The screeching terns which have been dive-bombing us all summer are long gone to a warmer climate. Everything looks grey and bare, and as the nights draw in, the clocks go back and Shetlanders settle in for the long, dark winter.

Many times we would battle our way to school against gale-force winds and rain, arriving soaked and cold. A westerly gale would usually blow itself out overnight, but at the first signs of a south-east gale, my father would declare: 'We're in for it now,' and the wind could blow for a week, building the sea into a frenzy of snow-white spindrift and massive waves which looked as if they were trying to smash our small island into submission. An awesome spectacle of Nature's powers. The lucky boats were in the harbour, and those that weren't would be out there fighting for their survival. The noise of the wind howling through the overhead wires, and the sound of the sea, was deafening. Heading down our street for school into the teeth of the gale was a hard job, usually two steps forward and one back, my lips tasting of salt spray.

Sometimes I lay in bed and listened to the house creak and groan, expecting the windows to be blown in. Occasionally, huge hailstones would hit the glass like shingle and thud on the roof, scaring the daylights out of me. If the same wind had swept across London, everything would have been flattened, but in Shetland anything that could blow away had done so years earlier.

During those early winter months we would start collecting wood and anything else that would burn on our Guy Fawkes bonfire. We combed the beaches and collected boxes and tea-chests from the shops and used tyres from the garages. In order to guard our efforts from the raids of opposing factions, we would build a wee gang-hut in the centre of the bonfire. How we weren't burnt to death I'll never know, sitting there with candles and sneaking the odd cigarette in the middle of that potential inferno. By the time the big night arrived, three or four huge bonfires would be ready to light up the night at South Lochside. No one really cared about fireworks: the roaring fires were fine and warm enough and often fairly spectacular. When they were reduced to burning embers, we threw in potatoes wrapped in foil to bake.

Those events were important during the long winters. They gave us something to look forward to and made life more bearable. Like most children, I started to get excited about the prospect of Christmas as soon as Guy Fawkes night had passed. Christmas Eve was without doubt the most exciting day of the year. As the time grew nearer, a whole new atmosphere came over the community. Even school became a happy place: the teachers would smile, and lessons became light-hearted. The build-up was unbearable. Neither we nor any of the other families had any money, but somehow no expense was spared for Christmas. Once the decorations went up, we knew that the festive season had really begun. Many loads of fir trees would arrive at the steamer store on the boat from Aberdeen. Ours was always a real tree, and once a year that beautiful pine smell filled the house. As Shetland had nothing in the way of trees, except some brave sycamores, it was a treat just to sit and gaze at the tree and admire its shape. My mother would start to bake cakes and sponges — her seedcakes, shortbread and bannocks were delicious. The house filled up with mouth-watering smells as she cooked her way through the week before Christmas.

Dad, with a glint in his eye, would top up his cupboard with various bottles, including Crabbies Green Ginger for his rum. Then there was Jimmy Shand and his Scottish country dance music — what would Christmas be without the people's favourite? The *Bluebell Polka* and *Whistlin' Rufus* would blare out of everyone's Dansette. I loved the dance music, and it seemed to fit into our lifestyles, especially at a time like Christmas.

When my brother and I were sent to bed on Christmas Eve, we lay there with our eyes wide open, desperately trying to fall asleep and hasten the arrival of Santa Claus, but still hearing the door open downstairs and the sound of laughter and merrymaking. The chimney stack went up through the corner of our bedroom, and when I was really young, my dad, knowing that I was awake, would put a stick up the lum and rattle it about to try to convince me that Santa was on the way down the chimney with our presents. I could never forget that feeling of joy and excitement, wondering if he had a spare pair of rollerskates or whether he had given them all away, and hoping he would like the whisky and cake we had left for him. It was always a worry as to whether or not he had received our letters that we had placed so carefully in the chimney weeks earlier. All would be revealed after we had gone to sleep, and that, of course, was the hard part.

Like all other children, we flew down the stairs on Christmas morning and there, under the tree, were our brown paper parcels tied with string. The knee-length woollen socks, hung by the fire, were full of apples, oranges, tangerines and nuts. Fruit was a great luxury — we rarely had it at other times of the year, except out of a tin.

Although my father hardly ever drank, he loved to indulge a little over the festive period. He used to pay a heavy price for his few whiskies. One year I went downstairs on Christmas morning to find him sitting with a basin between his feet. I said: 'Has he been?' — meaning Santa — and all he could do was point towards the tree.

Mother was wonderful at Christmas. The house was always spotlessly clean and shining, with the big peat fire giving it such a warm feeling. She was a traditional cook — never anything fancy, but always plenty of flavour. Uncle Andy would send us a hen for our dinner every year; a real hen, one that had lived outside and scratched its way around the land until chosen, plump for our Christmas. Then the stuffing: just a simple recipe of brown bread, onion, butter, salt and pepper. I've never tasted its equal.

Shetland cuisine comes into its own at Christmas, especially with the lovely fresh lamb from the hills, with a scent of heather in the meat. The favourite flavour of all at Christmas was the 'reested' mutton which hung from our clothes pulley. There it would dry and cure in the warm kitchen. The soup from the mutton is excellent and unique to Shetland. Into the boiling pot of mutton go onions, carrots, turnips, potatoes, and any other vegetables which can be found. Almost every house in Shetland would have a pot of reested mutton soup on the stove during the festive season. If anyone ever visited and looked in need of sustenance, out would come a bowl of soup, and the mutton would be cut off the bone and served with bannocks.

While Christmas was mainly a family affair, when I was very young it was celebrated more than New Year. As I grew up, this gradually changed, but in my early years, Christmas was the time when people who lived normally very quiet lives would come bursting in our door at any time of the day or night with a good dram aboard, and dance, sing, or play the fiddle. Whisky was expensive in those days and was measured out with great precision in small shot glasses, not sloshed about as it is today. Guising was also a tradition at Christmas. Someone arrived disguised and we would sit around trying to guess who they were. It was never hard, as we knew each other, and some familiar movement would give the game away. It was all a lovely time for us children, and the season would bring friends on the island closer together.

When I left school at the age of fifteen, I really had no idea what I was going to do, but I was so glad to be free that I didn't care. Many of the boys who had left would join the merchant navy – there were so many Shetlanders sailing the waters that they were known as the North Sea Chinamen. The thought of sailing round the world to exotic places was an exciting one for a young lad brought up on a remote island. Nevertheless, I had developed many interests by that age and there weren't enough nights to do my fishing or my music. I had become a fanatical badminton player at school, as my mother and father had been in their youth. It was a very popular sport on the islands, and almost every country district had a club in the village hall. I used to play at St Clements as many as three or four times a week during the winter. In the summer, I spent the whole time fishing and devoted what was left over to my music. So I soon went off the idea of going to sea – it would have been too hard a wrench to leave and give up all of my favourite interests.

Instead, I found a job as an apprentice baker with the Alexandria Baking Company, in Harbour Street. I had two uncles who were bakers – Peter, in Sandwick, and Bertie, my father's youngest brother, who lived in Prestwick. My great-uncle had owned one of the bakeries in Sandwick, and it seemed the right thing for me to do.

I was started on a trial period, and I loved the work. I had to begin at 4 a.m. to help with the early supply of bread and oatcakes which would be taken out to the country areas of the north in the bakery vans. It was summer, and I enjoyed the walks to work: everything was quiet and peaceful. The gulls resting in the playing park looked like snow in their numbers. Wanting them to wake up, too, I would throw a stone at them and imagine that I was waking the whole town from its slumbers as they rose in their screaming thousands.

I loved the smell of baking bread which greeted me as I arrived for work. There was plenty to do, and as the apprentice I never had a spare moment: cutting the dough, putting it in the greased tins and placing as many as possible in the ovens with the long, flat wooden shovels. I scraped the baking trays before greasing them ready for use and pulled up the ingredients for the next batch from the shop below. I remember the hatch well, because I blistered and bloodied my lily school hands. All the bakers who worked there were good to me, but I made special friends with two of them, Davy Pottinger and Maurice Hoseason, who were also keen fishermen.

When we were on early shift, we would leave work at two in the afternoon and cycle over to Maggie Black's Loch, about four miles from Lerwick. Within half a mile of the loch, we got off our bikes and walked over the hill. The loch could not be seen from the road, and to most people it looked like a deep puddle. However, as the fishermen well knew, its depths were home to some fierce brown trout. The water was so dark with peat that the fish could hardly see each other, and so fly-fishing was out of the question. Only what we called the garden lure – the ever-reliable worm – could reveal their presence. Cast out to the middle of the loch, attached to a bubble float and left to drift with the wind, the worm was deadly. We took many big fish, up to six pounds, from Maggie Black's Loch during our afternoons off.

I was earning £3 a week during my trial period. If I had been a fully paid apprentice I would have earned £1 more, a fact my employers had not overlooked. I soon realised that I was being exploited, and I handed in my notice – with regret.

I was soon back at work, this time in the county architects department, where my father worked. That was 1961, and my wages were one shilling an hour for a 42-hour week. I gave half to my mother and felt a surge of independence.

Having my father at the same workplace had both advantages and disadvantages. He was good at warning me when some of the older men were going to play a joke on me – as the apprentice, I was the prime target. On the other hand, my father had high expectations and kept his eye on me all the time. I was nervous, and I had little experience of woodwork. Worst of all, I was barely five feet tall. Growing was not one of my strong points. If I stood on a scaffold, I couldn't reach the ceiling; when I tried to saw wood, the stool would be too high and when I lowered the stool the saw would hit the ground. It was a nightmare. I couldn't even reach the workbench. I remember the men looking at me on my first day: they must have been wondering what on earth they were going to do with me. Fortunately, they were a nice bunch, and although one or two of them played the usual pranks – like sending me off to the store for sky hooks or a long stand – I was usually forewarned and avoided them. I was also awarded a few nicknames, like Sparrowlegs or Shortarse (I had big ears and I was once told that I looked like a Baby Austin with both doors open!). The only way was to fight back, so I gave as good as I got and soon settled down to serve my time.

My elation at leaving school was quickly doused, however, because my first job as a joiner took me back there to replace one of the classroom ceilings. It was a strange experience, being a free man back at school among the familiar teachers. If the headmaster, who put the fear of God into everyone, came to see how we were progressing I burnt my fingers putting out my cigarette before he noticed. I enjoyed this visit to the school as little as I had enjoyed all the previous ones.

My next assignment took me to Burravoe, on the island of Yell, with my father, Henry Hunter and Harry Smith. Our task was to replace the council house windows. I had hardly been away from home, and the north islands were like being abroad. We lodged with Lila and Andrew Hughson in Hamnivoe, only a mile or two from our workplace. It was late summer, the weather was beautiful and the landscape looked at its best. There was hardly a cloud in the sky for the two weeks we were there. Yell is the largest of the islands, apart from the mainland, and is almost completely covered in heather, beneath which lies an endless supply of peat. The heather was in full bloom, and, in the early hours as we cycled to work, the air was full of its fragrance, the sound of the shimmering sea and the best music in the world – sung to us by hundreds of skylarks.

On one of our free nights, we were invited to visit Brucie Henderson and his wife at Erisdale. Brucie was one of the best-known storytellers on the islands. A man of striking appearance, he had long white hair and his eyes looked off in different directions. You could never tell whether or not he was looking at you, and yet I was transfixed by his hypnotic effect – similar, I imagined, to that of Rasputin. His wife had prepared a gigantic meal of soups, bannocks and mutton. We ate so much that it was all we could do to haul ourselves over to the fireside afterwards.

Brucie then launched into a series of stories, most of which were Shetland versions of traditional tales about the devil and his many forms, and about the effects of the

Henry Hunter's retiral. Aly's father is behind Henry with all of Aly's workmates in the county architect's department

waning moon and the ebbing tides. Other stories were about his own encounters with the trows (Shetland's answer to the trolls) and how he had managed to outwit them. He told his tales with such conviction, remembering every detail, that it was hard to disbelieve him. I had my fiddle with me, and in between stories I played a few Shetland tunes. Henry Hunter, who was from Unst, had a few grand tales of his own and he loved to recite Shetland poetry. His favourites were *Mansie's Crö* and *Babbie Gullets Duke*. After each rendition, Henry would laugh and slap his knees. He loved to tell stories of strong men, of how when he was a young man at sea he had seen a huge Arab squeeze the bosun's hand until the blood ran from his fingertips. After every story, Henry exclaimed: 'My Goad, quat tinks du o' dat?'

My father loved poetry, too, and after a few drams he couldn't resist the urge to join in. His favourite poets at the time were Burns and Byron, so we listened to *The Cottar's Saturday Night* and *On this Day I Complete my 36th Year*. He loved the poems dearly, and certain lines would bring him near to tears.

As the night went on and the fire grew warmer, my father and Harry Smith started nodding and letting their heads fall forward, only coming to life when a fresh dram was offered. It was a night I'll never forget: looking back, it seems as if we were in a different century. We made our way home through the beautiful morning with the curlews calling overhead and me secretly keeping an eye out for trows.

Fortunately, I soon started to grow, and eventually reached my full height of five foot six and a half inches. I always insist on the half inch – it makes me feel better. It was the responsibility of our department to do all the maintenance on schools, hostels, county buildings and council houses throughout the islands. During the summers, we usually worked outside while the weather was half decent. During the winter, if we were lucky, the work was mainly indoors, and I enjoyed being at the workbench most. We had a big Bogie stove, always full of wood-cuttings. The workshop, which was at the north end of Lerwick, had hardly any machinery. At the beginning of my time there, everything was made by hand. We made doors, gates and windows. There was a fair amount of pride in the finished object: things were made to last, and the other joiners examined the work carefully, always commenting cynically on any mistakes. It was all in fun. As I walk around Lerwick today, I can still see that some of my handiwork has survived on the local authority buildings.

Coming from a political family where we frequently argued about and discussed all kinds of issues, becoming a working man meant more than just getting a job. All of my family were socialists, to the left of the Labour Party, and I had this naïve belief that all working-class people thought as we did. For me, it was very much an 'us and them' situation. However, when I started work I soon realised that this was anything but the case. Of the twenty or so men who were our workmates, only about three or four voted Labour, and only one of the joiners was in the union, the Amalgamated Society of Woodworkers.

My dad and I were the Ragged Trousered Philanthropists. I joined the union, and had visions of mass meetings and demonstrations. In fact, our meetings were held in a room above the Excelsior pub, and only me and two other people – Alex Manson, who

Brucie Henderson much as Aly remembers him at home in Airisdale, Yell. A wonderful storyteller and a hospitable host, he would begin all his tales with 'My name is Brucie Henderson and I live at the foot of a great big mountain.' The mountain, like the stories, had to be taken with a pinch of salt

worked with me, and Tammy Coutts, from another firm – ever attended. This situation led to some great arguments in the workshop. At the bench, I worked opposite Peter Moncrieff, the oldest member of our staff. He was from the Ness (the southernmost part of the mainland) and was a staunch Baptist and a true-blue Tory. His motto in life was that you couldn't be a millionaire if you were a ha'penny short. He never drank or smoked, although he chewed copious quantities of tobacco. All day long, every few minutes, he spat a stream of brown saliva underneath the bench among the wood-shavings. I used to dread cleaning out the shavings at night and coming across one of those hard brown blobs. I used to argue with Peter all the time about current affairs. He tried to avoid the impending argument by just working away, pretending not to be interested. I knew his sore points, though, and used to mumble to myself, knowing that he would erupt at some point. The other men in the workshop listened intently, waiting for the explosion.

More than anything else, Peter loved the Bible and Winston Churchill, and he never swore. Instead, he would exclaim 'By Gory!' or 'By Christopher!' or 'By Jacob!'. And instead of 'damn' he would say 'dwined'.

I suppose it became a challenge for me to get him to swear, so when the right moment came I would say: 'Well, as far as I'm concerned, Winston Churchill was an old bastard!' The fuse would reach the gunpowder: 'By Jacob! What dus du know aboot Churchill, du dwined arseless critter?' Off we'd go, tools were downed, and before long the whole company was up to its ears in a major argument. It was all great fun and tongue-in-cheek, making the day's work more bearable. Peter actually had a very dry Shetland sense of humour, and for all our jousting he and I were great friends.

Another character at work whom I mentioned earlier was Henry Hunter. Henry loved working with wood: he would touch the object he was crafting as a mother would her child. Speed was certainly low on his list of priorities. He loved the sound of his plane, which would whistle as he shaved away the wood. As soon as this noise stopped, he would remove the blade and sharpen it, which meant that most of his time was spent on this task. He would run his hand over the wood and say: 'Goad, feels du dat!' Every joint was made perfectly and soaked in paint against the weather. On finishing his work, he would admire it and say: 'Dis door 'ill be here lang after A'm geen.' He had a superb collection of tools, old and new, all ready and oiled for the next job. He was a charmer, too, and if we were working on the outside of someone's house during the winter, Henry soon had the housewife cooking bacon and eggs for our 'ten o'clock'.

I couldn't say I made an enemy of anyone in the eight years I worked as a joiner; even with our foibles we all got along very well. At Christmas, we all clubbed together and bought three or four roast chickens for our last afternoon at work, usually Christmas Eve. Starting at two in the afternoon, all the lads arrived at the workshop, most of them with a half bottle and some beer. We had fiddles and the guitar and made merry all afternoon. Mother used to dread the state that Dad and I would come home in.

I enjoyed all the fun we had together, and have no regrets over that part of my life. I was never a good joiner, because my heart wasn't really in the job. Music gave me a way into a different world, but my years as a joiner taught me how to get on with people and many other things in life which I'll never forget. It also gave me a special relationship with my father, who I knew both as a workmate and as a friend. He was an early riser and always had the fire on and my breakfast ready before work. I used to come whistling down the stairs. We would shine our shoes and sling our 'piece' bags over our shoulders and head off for another day.

PART II   KEYS TO THE HIGHWAY

I persuaded my parents to buy me a fiddle when I was eleven years old, back in 1957. I had been pestering them for ages. There was a fiddle player called Ian McAlpine who lived just around the corner from me who had one for sale. It was a three-quarter size copy of a Stradivarius and very well made. I remember the excitement I felt as I walked up the road to buy it with the £3 my father had given me clutched in my hand. Three pounds doesn't seem like much now, but it was half my dad's weekly wage. Ian had put it into perfect working order and he threw in a case and a bow for luck. He also gave me a few tips about how to hold it under my chin and how to hold the bow.

Early days with school friends Margaret Leith and Johnny Wiseman in Jackie Sinclair's house next to the Peerie Shop

My father could play one tune on the fiddle, *The Lovat Scouts*, so when I got home he tried his best to work his big fingers on the small fiddle. I was determined to get some sort of music out of it before the end of the night and eventually succeeded in learning *The Grand Old Duke of York* – all four notes of it. Next day, me and my fiddle were camped in the lobby, where I was to spend many hours over the next few years. My next tune was *There is a Happy Land*, which took hours of total concentration.

The first Scots tune I learned was from my next-door neighbour, Maggie Simpson, who was from the island of Yell and could play a few tunes. Her son, Bertie, played guitar and her daughter, Annie, the piano. Maggie taught me *The Rowan Tree*. I just couldn't believe I was playing real tunes, and after a few days I was totally hooked on the instrument.

I then started learning tunes off the radio and records. I remember learning *The Liverpool Hornpipe* and thinking that I had arrived at a major musical moment. It was the first real fiddle tune I had learned, and I realised that if I could teach myself how to play triplets I could use them in the second part of the tune. I remember well trying to figure out those damned triplets and how my wrist wouldn't produce them for me. I really needed help. Fortunately, my parents had begun to take notice of my efforts. They were both amazed at the amount of time I spent out in the lobby. Neither of them had ever seen me concentrate on anything in my life, except maybe fishing. They got in touch with Tom Anderson, and he invited me along to his house for a listen.

Tom lived at Queens Place in Lerwick with his wife, Babs. I knew her quite well, as she used to visit my parents regularly – a friendship formed from the old days when we lived at Market Street. We had never seen much of Tom. He was always busy with his music and his job as an insurance agent.

Babs met me at the door and showed me into Tom's little music room. It was the beginning of the longest friendship of my life. Tom arranged for me to have lessons once a week. Every Tuesday night, he would pick me up in his little green Ford Popular and take me round to his house. His interest at that time was mainly Scots music. I was introduced to strathspeys, slow strathspeys, marches, reels and slow airs.

Tom at that time was around fifty years old, not much older than I am now, and fanatical in his love of fiddle music. He looked quite awesome to me – a big man with huge wrists and hands. He always had to make an extra hole at the very end of his watch strap, and I still can't figure out how his fingers made room for themselves on the fiddle's fingerboard. He would be a bit fierce with me at times, but I quickly learned that his bark was worse than his bite. He was the perfect teacher, and his enthusiasm kept pushing me on. We became two friends completely involved in what we were doing.

I think I was his only pupil in those days. There were hardly any other young players in the islands at that time. I remember we started with the traditional reel, *The Deil Amang the Tailors*. I still play it exactly as he taught it to me, and have based every other reel I play on the same bowings. I recall him saying: 'No, no, no! Gie me yon thing here!' – each 'no' getting louder and louder. 'Start we' a doon bow an' feenish we' a doon bow! Is du blind?' Then: 'An' whin du gits ta yon bit in da second half, when du's crossin' da strings, dee wrist should be goin' clockwise.' To many people, this won't make much sense, but to me it was valuable information, enabling me to play fast and clean.

The most difficult tunes to learn are strathspeys. We spent many hours working on them. Tom was a great admirer of James Scott Skinner, the 'Strathspey King', who died in 1929, so it was mainly his bowings that we studied. Being young, all I really wanted to play were fast reels, but Tom insisted that I must learn the art of strathspeys. We'd spend hours on one tune, like *Tulchan Lodge*, by Skinner himself, taking it bar by bar and working out every bowing.

Tom had a magnificent collection of written and taped music, so we could listen to Skinner himself playing the tune and feel the drive he put into it. Tom was in touch with fiddle players all over Scotland and Ireland. Tapes were sent and received every week. His collection grew bigger – reels and reels of tape, packed into his little room. For me, it was paradise to be among the tape recorders, tapes, records and almost every worthwhile collection of Scots music. I was very fortunate to be in the right place at the right time.

We worked every Tuesday from 7 to 9 p.m. Then Babs would wheel in a little trolley with tea and sandwiches. She was a kind, gentle woman. And patient, too –

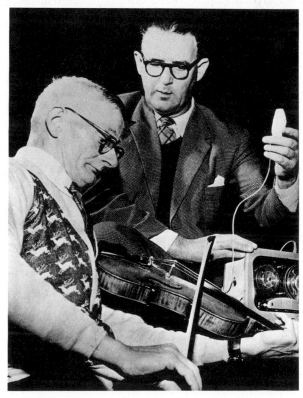

Tom tape-recording Alex Hughson, the oldest member of the
Forty Fiddlers

Aly (centre, back) hated his early classes with the classical teacher Geoffrey de Mercado, who attempted to cure his 'primitive' style—but failed.

having your life taken over by fiddle music couldn't have been easy at times. I remember her with great affection. They say that behind every great man is a great woman. I think that's rather insulting to women, but in her case I know she supported Tom to the hilt in his quest to keep our music alive.

When I got to be around thirteen, people began asking me to play at concerts and other local functions. I was horrified at the thought of playing to an audience, especially one full of familiar faces. I did everything possible to avoid playing in public. To make things worse, I had a bad stammer – mainly because of my problems with school – and sometimes I could hardly get two words out. The day I left school, the stammer virtually disappeared. Again, it was Tom who pushed me, always saying that it would be okay. Tom was a difficult man to argue with.

I remember going to school camp near Edinburgh. It could have been the moon as far as I was concerned. All of us who were from Shetland seemed to spend the whole time at that camp climbing trees – none of us had ever seen so many of them before. I took the fiddle with me because my classmates wanted me to. On the last night of the camp, they had a concert. Halfway through it, one of my friends told the MC that I could play. I was sitting in the audience, and he began shouting out my name. I spent the whole event underneath a chair, hiding from the man. I could see his feet next to me as he walked past looking for me. It was my first – and by no means last – case of severe stage-fright.

I was always to find it tremendously difficult to play the fiddle in public and for years I couldn't play slow airs because the bow would shake so much on the strings. I still have the same problem today, no matter where I am, and it's why I like to sit down when I'm on stage because my knees shake as well!

At the same time as I was getting lessons from Tom, a new teacher of classical violin came to Shetland. His name was Geoffrey de Mercado, and I decided to take lessons from him – mainly out of curiosity. I managed to get some periods off school to attend his class in the community centre in Isleburgh House. Geoffrey's family were Italian, and he was a trained violinist. He had worked as a musician in London before moving to Shetland to work at the weather observatory. He seemed to be able to do anything on the violin, and I was amazed, never having heard a classical player before.

I remember my first lesson with him very well indeed. After I had taken my fiddle out and was ready to begin, he said: 'Play for me.' So I played a Shetland reel called *The Merrie Boys of Greenland*. His reaction was one of horror.

'This is not music,' he said. 'This is rubbish. How can I teach you? You have started to play all wrong, and it's probably too late to save you.'

I sat there in shock. This was definitely a teacher of a different kind. I had met my first musical snob.

In his determination to show me how simple our music is, he would open the Scott Skinner book, *The Scottish Violinist*, and play the most difficult tune in the book as easy as falling off a wall. I was truly amazed, as I could hardly read music anyway. He played it flawlessly, but he never sounded in any way like a fiddle player, try as he might.

There was no doubt about his ability as a violinist. He entertained people all over the islands and became a weel-kent face. I was astonished at how much tone he could produce from the instrument. He had been trained, as every violinist is, to use every inch of the bow and pull out the maximum of power. Just sitting watching him play was an education. Although I went to him for only a short time, I learned a great deal from him about the mechanics of bowing.

There were days when the fiddle would fight back at me, when nothing would go right and it seemed to have a mind of its own. I would eye it up just like Frank Bruno does with an opponent as it lay in its case, the frustration reeling in my head, and say: 'Shite for dee!' and grab it again for another wrestling bout. Like all bowed instruments, the fiddle is a physical challenge, with everything going in different directions, slippery in your hands like an eel. One moment it would drive me into a white rage, the other into the depths of despair. At other times, when it decided to sing for you, all was forgiven and it was wonderful to feel in control. Nowadays, the fiddle mainly does what I want it to do, but when I am teaching children I sometimes try to remind myself how difficult it is in the beginning and play it left-handed. After the first few notes, all the bleak feelings come flooding back again.

In 1959 Tom Anderson formed the Shetland Fiddlers Society – or the Forty Frenzied Fiddlers, as Magnus Magnusson liked to call us. I was a founder member at the age of thirteen. Our first public performance was at the Hamefaring in 1960. It

Practising with the Forty Fiddlers for their first concert at the Hamefaring (1960)

was a big occasion. Shetlanders from all over the world came home for a celebration in their honour. Most were from New Zealand and Australia, where Shetlanders have traditionally emigrated to, but pockets of them came from all over the globe. A longship was built and burned afloat on the Clickimin Loch. The fiddlers gave a concert, and there were numerous other events. Eyes were full of tears as long-lost friends and families were reunited. The 'Old Rock' had drawn them home again, as it always does. I know the feeling well. People never really leave Shetland — a part of them always remains behind, and from time to time they have to reconnect.

The forming of the Fiddlers Society meant a great deal to me, as it brought me into contact with some of the best players in the islands and some of the greatest characters. My place on stage was beside Tom at the end of the front row, where he could keep an eye on me. Next to me sat Willie Pottinger and Willie Hunter senior, two of the best older players. Further along was Frankie Jamieson, our treasurer, known throughout the island for his playing and fine compositions.

For me, it was a wonderful experience. The players came from all over the mainland – the rest of the islands were at that time too remote. We had a practice every Wednesday night in Isleburgh House community centre. Tom was determined to knock us into shape and he selected all the music. He stood at the front, where he could see everyone. If someone made a mistake, he wouldn't say a thing; instead, he inflicted such a glowering glare on them that they visibly shrank out of view. It was Tom at his best. He was in total command, whether glaring or handing out compliments.

Tom was still quite young – in his early fifties. He had endless energy and drove the fiddlers on with his enthusiasm. I think he saw the society as a club where fiddlers could take refuge. He was also desperate to save the art from dying out. He gave the players new life in their music and had their undying loyalty. People who had hardly played for years blew the dust off their fiddle cases and showed up ready for action. They came from every walk of life – there were crofters, accountants, tradesmen, fishermen and, to keep things legal, we had the Procurator Fiscal.

Backstage before a concert was mayhem, with bows going in every direction and shouts of 'Soond an A'. Then there would be a roar from Tom, and silence. After the As were all tuned, it was time for the 'fly' inspection – to see that everything was zipped up in front. That was followed by a peerie toot from a half bottle, and then everyone headed for the stage. Sometimes the stage was on the small side, and fiddlers were crammed in every corner. Most of the time our poor pianist, Marjorie Smith, was stuck away at the side of the stage and never even seen by the audience.

The audience would sit through all the rumbling feet and scraping of chairs as we got on stage, separated by a thin curtain. Some of the remarks made by various fiddlers, as they tried to fit their chairs on to an area which seemed the size of a postage stamp, are unrepeatable in this book, but of course the audience could hear them through the curtain, and more often than not, would know the voices which uttered them and fall into fits of laughing.

Many of these utterings came from Willie Pottinger, who was the best-loved character in our society. Willie had been influenced in his early days by the Blind Fiddler from Dundee, George Stark, who made his living busking around Scotland. George Stark used to come to Shetland during the herring fishing season and busk in Lerwick and Scalloway. On his first visit, in 1901, he had a guitarist called Willie Jordan, and, according to Tom Anderson, that was the first time a guitar had been played on Shetland, bringing a new tradition to the islands. George Stark continued to visit Shetland until the late 1950s, by which time he was, of course, an old man.

Willie Pottinger met the Blind Fiddler on many occasions and learned his unique style of Scottish playing – not the polished style of today, but more earthy and real, full of raw feeling and character. It was music of the ordinary people, the fisherfolk and farmworkers of north-east Scotland.

During our concerts with the Fiddlers, three or four soloists would be asked to play

John Leask and Magnie Wylie, two of the Forty Fiddlers,
at the Hamefaring (1960)

Flies all buttoned! The Fiddlers in October 1961, with Ronald Cooper on piano and Sonny Morrison on guitar

Willie Pottinger, a great fiddler and a great character, playing the Stroh fiddle

a few tunes. Willie Pottinger was always featured. Usually among his tunes would be the march *The Balkan Hills*, a tune he had made his own. None played it better. Willie, who could have played the tune in his sleep, hardly ever made a mistake. However, one night during a concert on the Isle of Whalsay, his solo began to disintegrate and, much to everyone's amazement, he only managed to reach the end with a real struggle.

Later, when we asked him what had gone wrong, he said: 'I wiz playin' away fine, castin' me eye aboot da a'dience, when dae fell on some wife I coorted whin I wiz young. An', be Christ, she winked at me an' pit me a' tae hell.' Apparently, Willie had found a groupie.

I remember another time when we had as a guest player a woman from Scotland, Betty Henderson, who played *The Banks Hornpipe*, one of the more difficult tunes, as a solo. Willie was, of course, interested to hear her rendition and was peeking round the stage door, watching her perform. When she finished, he said: 'Be Christ, she can play. When she took da doon bow at da beginnin' she bloody disappeared in a clood o' rosit.'

Willie had the gift to render us all helpless with laughter without even trying. He was a staunch member of the Fiddlers and rarely missed a night. I spent many happy musical times visiting him and his wife, Cellie. Her maiden name was Bain, and she was related to me through both my grandfather's and grandmother's side of my father's family. Cellie played the piano and vamped in the old style. Not long before they died, I went to visit Willie, who was in bed recovering from an operation. I remember Cellie meeting me at the door and saying that Willie was resting and maybe I should come back later. All of a sudden, Willie shouted from up the stairs: 'Let the peerie boy in for a tune!' So, while she opened all the doors so that he could hear, I stood in the living-room and played him a few tunes.

Both Willie and Cellie died on the same day: Willie first, followed a few hours later by Cellie, who died from the shock of her husband's death. It was a black day, and our little community was thrown into grief. With Willie's death, the style of the Blind Fiddler almost disappeared. Now only Willie's neighbour from across his street in Lerwick, Jim Stewart, a fine player in his own right, carries on that unique style of playing. I believe, as do many others, that of all the many reels that Tom Anderson composed, his best one was for Willie, in the key of F, called *Pottinger's Reel*.

Another great player who was a regular attender at the Fiddlers Society was Willie Hunter senior. The two Willies always sat together during our concerts, but had very different styles of playing. Willie Hunter came from Nesting but spent most of his life in Lerwick, where he worked as a blacksmith and had his own smithy. As well as being able to play Scots and Irish music, he was steeped in our own Shetland traditional playing. To watch his effortless, fluent bowing technique was a pleasure. Willie must have been around sixty years old in the early days of the Fiddlers, and to me was always a quiet gentleman. When he played the fiddle, he brought the instrument to life. His solo was always a high point during the night. His son, Willie Hunter junior, carried on this great tradition, putting the fear of death into most fiddle players with his great

With three favourite musicians – 'great music, great times, a rare privilege': Violet Tulloch, Willie Hunter senior and Willie Hunter junior

command of the instrument.

Another character among the Fiddlers was Curlie Jamieson. Curlie came from the west side of Shetland, near Walls. He would make the long journey – about thirty miles – every Wednesday on his motorbike. He loved motorbikes and was a regular spectator at the Isle of Man TT races. The weather rarely stopped him from reaching Lerwick. Some nights he would arrive covered in snow, with his fiddle strapped on his back.

Curlie was a touch eccentric and spoke very quickly in his native dialect. I found it difficult sometimes to keep up with what he was saying. He was also quite mechanically minded and very much a do-it-yourself man. Long before Bob Dylan was a twinkle in his father's eye, Curlie had refined the art of playing the harmonica and guitar at the same time. He had invented his own little stand for the harmonica, fixed to the guitar with two clamps and tightened up with a pair of oversize wing-nuts. The fixture was none too beautiful to look at, but it worked perfectly. When it came to his turn for a solo, Curlie would lay down his fiddle, pick up the guitar with the harmonica attached and sing local songs in an older American country style, to the delight and amusement of the audience. He wasn't shy like most of us. In fact, once he got going, Tom had a hard time getting him to stop.

Tom also insisted that I, as the youngest member, should play a solo, which I did, and that Alex Hughson, as the oldest, should play one too. Alex was my friend. He and I were always the first to arrive every practice night – me, because I loved the acoustics of the room, and Alex just because he liked to be there early. He always referred to me as just Bain. Alex held the fiddle in the old-fashioned way, down on his chest, and managed very well indeed. For his solo, he always played a tune called *Lowrie Tarrel*, a Shetland version of the Scots reel *The Mason's Apron*. The situation with Alex always proved a bit of a dilemma for Tom because Alex wasn't really the oldest member. That distinction went to Hughie Cummings, from Walls. Hughie was an infrequent attender, but might show up at any time for a practice or a concert, putting Alex into second place. Hughie must have been well through his seventies in those days, and his fiddling had seen better days; he was not totally in control of his bow. He also had a tendency to play at his own speed, regardless of what the rest of us were doing. Another unusual feature of Hughie's playing was that he mumbled to himself when he played. This mumbling could get quite loud if he got excited.

Tom lived in fear that Hughie would turn up on some important occasion, like when the Queen or some other dignitary would pay our islands a visit. Tom would have to change his introduction for Alex to 'one of our oldest members', which never sounded as good as 'the oldest'.

But what really threw Tom into a visible sweat was the fact that Hughie always finished a few seconds after the rest of us. While we all completed each set of tunes together, with a nice, crisp ending, Hughie would linger on for a few seconds, mumbling and playing, before reaching his own final chord, which was often only

Two great Shetland fiddlers, Bobby Jamieson and Willie Henderson from Yell (1970)

vaguely related to the key we were playing in. For a perfectionist like Tom, this was a nightmare. Nevertheless, he always welcomed Hughie and made him feel at home.

When I think back on those days, they were among the happiest of my young life, although I didn't realise it at the time. There I was, thirteen or fourteen years old, surrounded by all these characters and great players. Not one of them would hesitate to teach me anything I wanted to know. And on top of that, I got a few sips of beer on the way to a concert. Playing with them taught me not only about fiddle music but, more importantly, where it came from. I began to realise that music was an extension of the person. Each one played in his own way, according to his or her personality. They also taught me, through their stories and tales, a great deal about the islands I lived in and the kind of people I shared them with.

Had it not been for Tom Anderson, the Shetland Fiddlers Society would never have existed. He alone was the inspiration. Many of my fondest memories of Tom are from those times. In a way, he was much more open during that period in his life to all kinds of music, and was so full of fun.

During my visits with Tom during the last years of his life – he died in 1991 in his eighty-first year – we would reminisce about the early days. Tom, who knew all the players and characters so well, could mimic their actions and voices and have the company in fits of laughter.

At the same time as I was playing with the Fiddlers, I joined the Shetland Folk Society band, which had been formed in 1945. The idea had come from a committee formed in 1944 to present a concert of purely Shetland music and song. It was at this concert, in the Town Hall, that the band first performed. Within its ranks were many of our best players, including Willie Hunter senior, Willie Hunter junior, and John Pottinger. The band leader was Willie Anderson. I wouldn't have minded hearing that first concert.

The formation of the Folk Society came at a very important time. When the war finished in 1945, people looked to the future and a new way of life. There was a tendency to forget the past. This trend applied to music as well as to everything else. Council houses went up all over Lerwick, changing the town completely. A whole generation of young men and women who were my father's age came home from the war, having been exposed to different cultures and new ideas. I grew up to the sounds of Jimmy Shand. The radio was at the height of its influence. Record players became part of the furniture in most houses, and the records played on them were mainly from Scotland. Our music was pushed aside to make way for the new.

I remember my father telling me of a winter he had spent working at the school in Skerries just after the war, and teaching the locals new dances, like the Lancers and the Eightsome Reel. The old Shetland Reel, danced at one time all over the island, was quickly forgotten (though not in Skerries) and now is rarely danced at all.

The introduction of new music to the islands was a great thing. But at the same time, had it not been for the Shetland Folk Society, Tom Anderson and a few like-minded people, we would have lost much more of our rich heritage than we did.

There were others, too, from outside the islands who collected and preserved many

Waiting for the cue to record the Fiddlers' first TV programme, BBC Scotland's Da Peerie Isles, *which inaugurated the Bressay transmitter. The producer, Finlay J. Macdonald, is standing with Tom*

of our fiddle tunes. One man in particular, Pat Shuldam Shaw, an Englishman who worked closely with the English Folk and Dance Society and the School of Scottish Studies in Edinburgh, collected hundreds of tunes during the late 1940s which would otherwise have been lost.

In 1950 I was four years old and can remember little of the early part of the decade, but I do recall the impact of rock and roll. If you had looked through a typical record collection in Shetland during the early 1950s you would have found records by Ruby Murray, Michael Halliday, Doris Day, Jimmy Shand, Robert Wilson, Will Starr and so on, plus a large number of American country records. Country music has always been popular in Shetland, and Hank Williams was as much a part of my life growing up as Jimmy Shand was.

The record for me which changed everything was Bill Haley's *Rock Around the Clock*. All of a sudden, this new music arrived, exciting and different. The record industry took off. Out went Doris Day and in came skiffle, Little Richard, Elvis, Fats Domino and Roy Orbison, sweeping our generation on into the 1960s and all that followed.

Among my age group, fiddle music was hardly the 'in' thing, and it has always amazed me that I managed to take up the instrument at such a time. Overnight, everyone wanted to look like Elvis. I remember my brother combing back his black hair, all sleeked with Brylcreem, and trying to get rid of the wee white specks of dandruff.

In the middle of all this, I felt a bit odd going to fiddle lessons, with my fiddle case by my side – I would try to hide it, or make it look as if it really didn't belong to me and I was only delivering it for somebody else. For all that, I couldn't give it up. I must have got the bug.

Playing fiddle didn't stop me loving all the other kinds of music going on around me. The problem was that very few of my generation felt like I did. There was only a handful of us playing, and interest in traditional music had pretty much reached rock-bottom. There was at that time a real chance of it dying out, with hardly anyone left to carry on the tradition. There were a few players older than me, but things looked bleak for the future.

I think the same thing was happening in Ireland. Cathal McConnell, my colleague in the Boys of the Lough, remembers the '50s as a particularly lean time for traditional music there.

This negative attitude to all things traditional was also reflected in our education. Music tuition at secondary school was pretty much non-existent. Our native dialect was discouraged and frowned upon. While being able to recite the accession to the English throne by heart, we knew little of Scots history and even less about Shetland's. I doubt if any pupils at that time would have known the date when Shetland ceased being a part of Norway.

In the early days, when I was working with Tom and just before I left Shetland, there was very little interest in the music. Happily, it's a very different story today. Since the mid-1970s, interest has been building up in Shetland's traditional culture generally and fiddle music in particular. There are some great young players, and more are coming up all the time. That's mainly due to Tom Anderson's work in teaching and stimulating people. Once Tom got something on his mind, then nothing in hell would stop him. He decided he was going to teach, and it should be in schools, and it was when he got the teaching into the schools as a normal part of the curriculum that it really started to work. If you had the option, will I take religious studies or will I go to Tom and learn the fiddle? then there was no question about it. He had more pupils than he could ever handle, and so they had to hire extra teachers. Now there's three or four going round the schools and there's maybe 150 or 160 young people learning the fiddle in Shetland – which is great.

During the winter months, it was badminton and music that took up all my time. I loved badminton, and I played three or four nights a week at St Clement's, an old church in St Olaf Street. I think I just sort of strayed into the game. My pal Eddie Hutchison and I went along one night to see what was going on, and we ended up hooked. My mother had been a good player, so maybe it was in my blood.

There were about twenty of us who were the hard core of the game in Lerwick, although there were many other clubs throughout the islands. Eddie and I, along with others our own age, were determined to be selected for the Shetland team. I took this so seriously that music almost went out of the window. We eventually succeeded after

Rehearsing with Willie Anderson for a Fiddlers' concert in the Garrison Theatre (1962)

a few years and got to play for the team in its annual game against Orkney. The great players of my time were Tiny (Tommy) Jamieson, Pundy (George) and Ruby Smith, Rob Anderson, Do Do (George) Burgess, Duncan Robertson, Stanley and Margaret Sinclair, Kenny Rae and Bill Moar. We were all friends, and spent many happy hours together.

The flight with the team to Orkney was the first I had ever made – and it was a feeling I won't ever forget. We always lost the inter-county game in Kirkwall, basically because they had a terrible hall to play in, but the party afterwards was something else, win or lose. We had great women players, too. Rob Anderson played with Hilda Hunter, Stanley and Margaret got married and became almost invincible, and I played with Joan Williamson, who was a giant compared to me – when she played at the net, I had no idea where the shuttle was going until it passed her. We may never have reached the heights of international standard, but we tried our best.

Music, of course, was the other major thing in my life. During the early days with the Fiddlers Society, I had met Ronald Cooper, who played piano with us on many occasions. We became great friends. Ronald was always up for a tune. Indeed, he was a complete fanatic when it came to music. Around the time I was fifteen, the Hayfield Hotel in Lerwick was the place in Shetland for music. The hotel was owned by Frank Chadwick and his wife Lillian, who was Ronald's first cousin. Ronald was really into Scottish country dance music, a subject he knew more about than anyone else. He was familiar with every band and every musician. Whenever there was a band from the mainland touring in Shetland, they would always stay at the Hayfield, and, of course, we would meet them and play into the wee hours.

During this period, Ronald was composing many tunes. He seemed inspired. Tunes seemed to roll off his fingers – great tunes like *Da Tushker*, *Calum Donaldson* and *Susan Cooper*, named after his daughter. In all, he produced sixty or seventy tunes within a few years, all of which were snapped up by the visiting bands. Soon his tunes could be heard on the radio every week, and his name became known throughout the world of dance music.

The Team. Aly's last year in the centre courts before the match against Orkney ('We won!'): Back row (left to right): Duncan Robertson, Gordon Bolt, Kenneth Rae, Aly, Rob Anderson, Stanley Sinclair, Front: Caroline Smith, Sheena Forbes, Muriel Eunson, Joan Williamson, Hilda Hunter, Margaret Leith (St Clement's Hall, March 1968)

Ronald and I had great times together. As well as being a wonderful musician, he had a great sense of humour. We had our own dance band, along with Erik Cooper (accordion, no relation), Jack Robertson (bass), Bobby Ganson (drums) and Jimmy Henry (guitar) and played at dances all over the islands. God, we had some laughs.

During those years I played in many bands with various musicians. We got paid £1 per night – easily doubling my wages as a joiner. I also made my first recording with Ronald. It was a little EP called *Reflections from Shetland*, and was made on a tape recorder belonging to Drew Robertson. Our main regular session was every Saturday lunchtime in the Lounge pub, which is now famous throughout the world of traditional music. Ronald and Erik Cooper had been playing there for years. I used to listen outside the window before I was old enough to get in, and I would envy the sounds ringing from up the stairs. When I became eighteen, wild horses couldn't have kept me out. Only good musicians were allowed to sit in. If anyone was below par they were diplomatically told to keep quiet. Without hardly knowing, they would get the vibes, pack up their instruments and drift away. Ronald and Erik, each swapping between accordion and piano, were totally in charge. The music was wonderful. Many of the great players from the islands and further afield would drop in for a tune. Sometimes the roof seemed as if it would be blown away by the music. I think I learned more about music during those times than I have ever learned.

Little did I know when Ronald and I played together for the BBC in Ollaberry in 1966 how much my life would be changed by music. I still play in the Lounge when I go back to Shetland, although Ronald, sadly, is long gone. He died when he was only in his forty-eighth year. Shetland to me can never be quite the same without him, although the Lounge, run by locals Hughie and Jemima Robertson, is still going strong with its Saturday lunchtime sessions. To me, it has always been the one truly Shetland pub in Lerwick.

Many families on the islands are broken up early when sons and daughters have to leave for university or to find work. Many of them never return to live in Shetland again. My brother, Douglas, went to Aberdeen University, and my sister, Anne, was soon to follow. My parents hoped that I would stay home and start a family. My father and I had worked together for eight years, so it looked as if things were settled. When I told them I was leaving, they were deeply hurt, because it meant they were losing all of us. The strength in our family was that we as children respected our parents. We all knew how much they had sacrificed to bring us up. They, in turn, had the courage to change as we grew up and became part of our new world. They supported us all in everything we did in life.

During the early years, after I left Shetland, when I teamed up with Mike Whellans, we worked a lot in England, and I used to stay in Newcastle with Tommy and Maggie Gilfellon. Tommy was a member of the High Level Ranters band, whose music was very akin to our own. They were *the* formidable force and standard-bearers of traditional music in the north-east of England. Tommy and Maggie, whose house became a refuge for wandering minstrels, looked after me on many occasions. My mother at that time was convinced that I was dying of starvation, and took to posting

With Ronald Cooper and Willie Johnson in Aly's parents' house after sister Anne's wedding

me legs of lamb. Tommy would answer the door and shout: 'Here's another sheep for Aly!' I don't know how many sheep she sent me over the years, along with jumpers and a host of other things. My parents were the only sponsors I ever had.

Leaving Shetland was the most difficult thing I have done in my life. I remember to this day the knot in my stomach and the feeling of nausea as I stepped on to the plane. For the first time in my life, I felt truly alone.

Shetland is a changed place since I left. At that time, the oil industry was in its early development. Whatever fears we all had, there is no doubt that the oil has brought prosperity to the islands. Lerwick has expanded beyond all belief. There is a new generation of Shetlanders whom I hardly know. Both of my parents have died, and our old house in Russell Crescent is no longer a part of my life.

I made a promise to myself that I would never lose touch with the islands, and I never have. I go back as often as I can — usually three or four times a year. My sister, to the joy of my parents, moved back to work in Shetland. Sometimes I stay with her, and when I am in Lerwick I stay with my great friends Violet and Drew Tulloch. In my heart, I will always be a Shetlander.

Aly Bain
1993

Chapter Three

TAKING A BOW

Emigration can never be easy. It's all the harder when you love your family, your friends and your native soil in the way that Aly did. Many of his pals were baffled by his decision to leave in 1968. And, in truth, he himself wasn't entirely convinced that he was doing the right thing. There he was, at twenty-two, living a life that could have gone on happily ever after, playing top-notch badminton three times a week, fishing the trout-filled lochs through the spring and summer, and making music with Tom Anderson's group as well as in a dance band at weekends with the pianist Ronald Cooper. As a time-served joiner, he was also doing a job of work which may not have offered much in the way of stimulation or riches but which was his, if he wanted it and if he kept his nose moderately clean, until he started picking up his old-age pension.

'I had this great life. I never imagined I would ever leave. I had so much to cram into a week, my parents never saw me.'

But a number of different strings were beginning to tug naggingly at his peace of mind. Not least of these was sheer curiosity. 'I felt that if you lived all your life in Shetland and never left it, then you'd never know . . . I couldn't really exist without knowing what went on in Scotland.'

For Aly, and for many Shetlanders, mainland Scotland was almost foreign territory, one of those faraway places with strange-sounding names and even stranger ways of living. 'All I knew about Scotland was that it was a big country with cities and trees and things, and I wanted to go and experience it.'

Apart from his expedition to Edinburgh for school camp, he had already paid a couple of fleeting visits to the Big Country, enough to whet his appetite for more. In 1964 he went to Glasgow for the wedding of his brother Douglas. It was on that trip that Aly was taken along to the folk club which had sessions every week in the Grand Hotel at Charing Cross. There, he found something he had never even dreamed of: a room packed with young folk enthusiasts, singers and musicians – among them, Archie Fisher, Josh Macrae and Hamish Imlach – and an audience that seemed strangely content to sit and listen rather than get up and dance. That night, Aly plucked up the courage to play a few tunes. For many of the crowd, it was a revelation:

great music of a type that they had never heard before, played by a brilliant fiddler of their own generation.

At the end of his set, one of the first people to grab his arm and shake him by the hand was Billy Connolly, who at that time was getting to be known as a banjo player who sang mainly American country songs and who was beginning to display a decided gift for an outrageous brand of hilarious blether. Aly hadn't the foggiest idea who this person was in the outlandish hippy clothes, long hair and straggly beard, but 'I remember him stopping me and saying he loved what I'd done. He's not the kind of guy you forget in a hurry.'

The feeling, it appears, was mutual. Connolly never forgot the sensation of hearing Aly's music for the first time. Later, he played a major role in establishing the Shetland fiddler on the folk scene, and they have remained great friends ever since.

But in the meantime, Aly was still blissfully unaware that there was a solid audience for his music, apart from a few dedicated folk *aficionados*, and he went home to Shetland, as he puts it, 'to get on with my life'.

Three years later, Archie Fisher, whose fine singing and guitar playing had put him firmly in the vanguard of the Glasgow folk revival, was instrumental in arranging for Aly to play as a featured guest at the second Blairgowrie traditional music festival. Aly saw it as a bit of a jaunt, something to break the Shetland routine, and once again it amounted to a brief encounter with the folk scene. This time, though, he got his first real inkling that 'something was indeed happening musically down in Scotland'.

At Blairgowrie he met and heard for the first time Christy Moore, the Irish singer and songwriter who was to go on to form the influential Planxty group, and another Irishman who was to become one of his greatest friends and musical mentors, Finbar Furey, an outstanding Uillean piper. Also at Blairgowrie were some of the great Scottish traditional singers and musicians of an older generation who had been tracked down by the indefatigable Hamish Henderson and his colleagues at the School of Scottish Studies — notably Jeannie Robertson, the supreme ballad-singer once described by the American folklorist Alan Lomax as 'a monumental figure of the world's folksong', and Willie Scott, the singing Border shepherd.

'When I saw all those people who loved traditional music and liked what I did, I was just amazed,' says Aly. 'These were people I could relate to. I had a great time. I would do my bit and then go into the pub and get wellied into the drams and have a great night of songs and music.'

Aly, somewhat to his alarm, found himself sharing a double bed in a house with Willie Scott. The room next to them was occupied by Jeannie, her fiddler husband Donald, and Donald's brother Isaac, who played the pipes. 'Willie, being a shepherd, used to get up at the crack of dawn and would hobble off downstairs and bring me breakfast – a nip of whisky and a half pint.'

Then Aly would make a proper breakfast for Jeannie and her clan. 'All you'd ever hear them say was "Oh God A'michty!" I'd knock on their door and they'd say, "Oh God A'michty!" I'd say I'd brought them some breakfast and they'd say, "Oh God

A'michty!'', and I'd take in the tray and say I'd see them later and they'd say it again: "Oh God A'michty!".'

That Blairgowrie festival was an eye-opener for Aly, although he still couldn't see the potential that the folk scene offered him. 'I met one or two fiddlers, like Bob Hobkirk from the Borders and John Mason from Orkney, of fiddle rally fame, but there weren't many fiddlers on the scene then – maybe half a dozen. So I was a bit of a novelty as far as the public were concerned. Here I was going into the heartland of Scotland and finding that all these people had never heard their own fiddle music before.'

Blairgowrie attracted folk fans from Edinburgh, Glasgow and the other cities, where singers and singer-songwriters were very much in vogue. Traditional instrumental music was hardly played in the urban folk clubs, although Finbar Furey was beginning to make an impression. So Aly viewed Blairgowrie, run by a small group of revivalists who had formed the Traditional Music and Song Association of Scotland, as a kind of one-off phenomenon. 'It was an inspired idea. For the first time, all these people with a common ground could get together in this beautiful place and make music. The residents, of course, hated it – an army of odd young people invading their peace and quiet. They finally stopped the festival being held there.'

Duncan Lunan, founder of the Irvine Folk Club, well remembers first hearing Aly at Blairgowrie during a session in the bar of the Victoria Hotel. Among the all-star cast were the Clutha, Mick Broderick, Ted Furey, Davie Stewart, Jimmy MacBeath and fiddler John Lincoln. Charlie Muir, from Brisbane, who was Lunan's second in command at Irvine, was there, too. 'It was incredibly hot,' Lunan recalls. 'The pub was so crowded that the doors had been closed. Charlie Muir was sitting on the windowsill, with one leg dangling outside, and he called across to me: "Hey, Dunc, there's a bloke with a fiddle out here." I said: "Well, let's have him in, Charlie." And in came the bow and the fiddle, followed shortly by that year's shy newcomer, Aly – by the scruff of the neck, as I remember. John Lincoln very quickly tried to overawe him, and there followed what amounted to a flyting, with John challenging Aly to play one piece after another and Aly rising to the occasion. I wish I'd recorded more of it, as that would have been a really historic record.'

Lunan was so impressed by Aly's playing that he persuaded him to take a gig at the Irvine Folk Club in the Sun Inn a week or so later. 'I knew it would go well, because the Irvine members were much into instrumentalists. We arranged for Aly to play for the sum of £5, which was in the kitty at the time. What I hadn't allowed for was that it was Marymass Festival Week. Josh Macrae, Matt McGinn and Hamish Imlach were appearing at the Harbour Arts Centre that night, admission free, so only about a dozen people turned up at the club. Aly was pretty nervous and he abandoned several tunes halfway, saying: "That isn't any good," while the rest of us were saying: "Yes it is, play on!"

'At the end of the night, Aly didn't want to take the fiver because there had been such a poor turn-out. But, of course, I insisted, and as far as I know that was the first time he had been paid for a booking. As we were packing up, Charlie Muir's cousin,

Keith Festival (1976). With singers Charlie Murray (second on left), Willie Scott (third on right), Belle Stewart and Willie Mackenzie (right) in the Seafield Hotel

Where did he get that suit? Aly with Margaret Bennett and Mike Whellans at the Blairgowrie Festival (1969)

*First professional booking at Irvine (1968). The
fee was £5, and Aly was reluctant to take it, as he
didn't think he had played well*

Mel Adam, said to me: "There may not have been many here, but this is your night —
that guy is brilliant."'

Yet again, Aly returned to Shetland and his joiner's workbench. After boozy
Blairgowrie, with its great 'crack' and music-making, it was all a bit of a comedown
and he began to feel distinctly restless. For a start, he experienced a severe dose of job
dissatisfaction. In those days, wages in Shetland were far below the national norm.
When he began working with the county architects department, he earned a mere £2 a
week, which his employers had carefully calculated at the rate of one and seven-eighth
pennies an hour — 'the miserable bastards could have paid me the other eighth of a
penny'. He gave half to his mother every pay-day. And yet, for a dance gig with the
band he got £1 in his pocket; two gigs in one week meant that he had doubled his
earnings and had some fun into the bargain. Years later, as a time-served joiner, his
wage amounted to only £11 — it took him three years to save up enough to buy his first
battered second-hand car.

'I was very happy except for the eight hours a day I was working. I wasn't a good
joiner. I wasn't going to get to be a foreman. And I would look at my dad and see me as
him in thirty years time, going out with my piece-bag every morning to do this job I
didn't like doing. It was different for him — he made the best of it, because he actually
enjoyed working with his hands. But he could see it was futile as well.'

Like many of his generation of Shetlanders, Aly's father had been away on war service and he also travelled to the big herring ports like Yarmouth in England to ply his coopering trade. He had seen a bit of the world, and had not been greatly impressed by what he saw.

But for Aly, the urge to leave finally became overwhelming. What clinched it was the vague prospect of working as a professional musician, somewhere, somehow. He had no clear idea what was out there; none of his musical colleagues in Shetland had ever taken such a dramatic step into the great unknown. But Aly reckoned that even if things didn't work out, he could always return home to earn a living as a joiner, and at least he would have made the effort.

It was on Arthur Argo's insistence that Aly left Shetland. Argo was in a good position to help the young fiddler, having set up a little agency that booked performers into folk clubs in both Scotland and England. He was already doing good business with Billy Connolly, Barbara Dickson and the Bitter Withy group.

Another friend who was pestering him to move south was Don Whyte, a Glasgow-based journalist and fanatical fisherman, who had met and heard Aly on angling trips to Shetland. Whyte, however, knew a lot less about folk music than he knew about fish: he actually saw a rosy future for Aly amid the tartan shenanigans of Scottish theatreland and, with the best of intentions, fixed up Aly's audition for *The Lex McLean Show* at the Pavilion Theatre in Glasgow, described at the start of this book. The salmon which caught the producer's eye on that occasion, as it lay strapped to Aly's fiddle case, was in fact a thank-you present for Don Whyte.

Aly had caught the salmon on his last full day in Shetland before boarding the plane to Aberdeen – a day that he recalls now as one that almost made him change his mind about leaving. 'I was to be best man at the wedding of Stanley Sinclair, and Margaret Leith, two of my badminton pals. Stanley was nervous about getting married, and I was nervous about leaving Shetland. So we decided to go fishing at five o'clock on the morning of the wedding to see if it would settle us down.'

The weather had been wild during the night – and in Shetland that means at least a gale-force wind. But the nervous groom and the nervous emigrant woke up at four o'clock to find a beautiful, clear day. They picked up their Milbro spinning rods, dug some worms out of the garden, and headed for Laxo, one of Shetland's finest salmon and sea-trout spots – 'Laxo' is in fact Norse for 'salmon'. At Laxo, the otters were at play, teasing each other by rolling down the river-bank and drifting to the point where the falls began. Aly and Stanley sat and watched this delightful scene for a while until the idyll was shattered by the arrival of a serious, Barbour-jacketed angler, festooned with all the latest fly-fishing gear. He began fishing from the opposite side of the burn with the kind of impeccable technique that can only be acquired from a library. The otters fled, and Aly and his pal made their first humble casts into the frothing waters.

Aly recalls: 'I threw my worm right up into the falling water. When it got to the bottom it stopped, and I thought, oh Christ, it's got hooked in on a wire or something. But it was a nine-pound salmon.'

Aly had to borrow a telescopic landing net from the expert fisherman to pull it on to the bank. 'Almost immediately, I caught another nine-pounder, and then another. Meanwhile, my friend threw in his worm and got a huge salmon, which broke his rod.'

The expert, having drawn a blank, was not particularly amused by all of this. 'His face got redder and redder and then purple,' says Aly. 'Then he swore at us, packed up his gear and hopped into his Land-Rover and left.'

It was the best day's fishing Aly had ever had, and it left him feeling so elated that he was sorely tempted to abandon his departure plans and settle for more mornings like this one. At the same time, though, he saw it as a good-luck omen – 'It seemed to be saying it's the right time to leave.'

Stanley Sinclair had to drag Aly away from the river that morning, and after the wedding the honeymoon-bound bride and groom caused some raised eyebrows at Sumburgh Airport when they were joined by the best man on the flight to Aberdeen.

Aly caught the train there for Glasgow. The whole business of rail travel – buying a ticket and finding the right train at the right platform – was still an unnerving experience for him, and when he reached Glasgow he felt as if he had climbed a mountain. He headed straight to the Pavilion Theatre for his audition, which brought him down from the mountain-top with a thump. 'At that point, I realised I wasn't going to get a job in the theatre – or maybe anywhere else for that matter.'

He went to stay with his brother, who had moved to Glasgow several years previously. Douglas worked for the Communist party. 'He had gone to Aberdeen university from Shetland and got involved in politics there,' says Aly. 'My father was very left-wing, and so was my mother. But when Douglas came back from university, we could see that he had changed, and my parents were horrified when they found that he'd joined the CP. He must have been the only member in Shetland at that time. As the years went by, my mother also joined the party, but my father and I never did.'

Aly had always felt that he was a political outsider in Shetland, where people tended not stray too far from the Jo Grimond concept of nice Liberalism. The bustling political life of Glasgow, where young activists were fighting for causes with the same commitment that Rangers or Celtic fans reserved for football, came as an invigorating surprise to Aly, so much so that he recalls an acute feeling of inadequacy in his role as a mere musician. 'It didn't seem to me you could make any statement playing the fiddle. It wasn't like getting up to sing about the miners as Dick Gaughan does. So I guess what was forming in my mind was that in order to make a statement in music it would have to be a cultural statement, because music and culture go hand in hand.'

That was the start of the Bain mission that drives him to this day. It was in Glasgow in the 1960s that he first became both alarmed and angered by television's depiction of Scottish culture as little more than a tame tartan hoe-down. 'Why weren't we hearing the real music?'

It was to be many years before television in Scotland reluctantly turned its cameras on to the 'real music', notably the music of Aly Bain. Meanwhile, though, Aly's more immediate task was to find a way of surviving in the big city, and the first few weeks were not encouraging. He was not only short of cash but also painfully homesick – 'What I really missed was my friends, even more than I missed Shetland. Everybody knew me there, and I knew everybody.' The traffic-clogged city streets were a nightmare, and the transport system never ceased to baffle him: in all his time in Glasgow, he only ever mastered one bus route – the one which delivered him safely to the Scotia Bar, favoured hang-out of the city's folkie gang.

The musical road was tough going at first, too, but things began to happen after Arthur Argo arranged for him to play at the Irvine Folk Festival, where Billy Connolly and his guitarist pal Tam Harvey were topping the bill as a duo called the Humblebums. Aly, whose repertoire at the time consisted largely of scintillating jigs and reels, 'played at three hundred miles an hour', proved to be one of the hits of the weekend, and the jungle bodhrans of the folk scene were soon spreading the message from Ayrshire to the powerful little band of folk-club organisers up and down Scotland. Irvine was an important milestone in another way – it gave Aly and Billy Connolly their first chance to get to know each other. Not long afterwards, as Billy explains in Chapter Six, Aly became an honorary member of the Humblebums.

Back in Glasgow, Billy Connolly swept Aly into a mad whirl of music-making, late-night drinking and irrepressible hilarity. 'Coming from Shetland, where people have a very dry sense of humour, I'd never met anyone as wildly funny as Billy before. He was a wild man in those days – larger than life – and everywhere we went you could see he had this amazing charisma. We knew even then that he was going to be a huge star.'

After closing time at the Scotia Bar, the doors would be locked and the fun would start, with Connolly and Mick Broderick, another great Glaswegian humorist, vying with each other to invent the funniest, most ridiculous stories. 'I've seen us lying on the floor, helpless, with tears running down our faces,' says Aly. 'That was the funniest I ever heard Billy, and it was long before he became famous. At that time, he seemed to be just incapable of saying anything that wasn't funny.'

The idea in those Scotia sessions was for Connolly or Broderick to pick on an object – it might be a cigarette packet or a pound note – and make a story out of it. For example, there was a helpful pole in the bar for weary customers to cling on to, a bit like a fireman's pole. One night, Mick picked up two empty beer cans and held them up to the pole, pretending it was a submarine periscope. And so began an epic, half-hour parody of wartime manoeuvres that Mick Broderick eventually went on to perform to great acclaim in the folk clubs. One year, he did his party piece in the traditional storytelling competition at the Kinross Folk Festival and was promptly disqualified, as Mick put it, on the grounds that the audience was sore with laughing.

For every great Broderick tale, Connolly would have another, even wilder than the one before. Those after-hours comic jousts in the Scotia Bar were like the formative sparring sessions in the career of a world champion boxer. They taught Billy how to think fast on his feet and deliver the knockout punchline. He was, as Aly had spotted, bound for glory.

But Connolly had some teaching of his own to do. The raw young Shetlander was not what you might call streetwise; he knew next to nothing about handling himself on stage as a professional musician, and his name as yet meant nothing to the folk-club punters. Billy persuaded the other half of the Humblebums duo, Tam Harvey, that it would be a good idea if they took Aly on board and showed him a thing or two. 'On board' meant Aly climbing on the back of Billy's motorbike, with Tam in the sidecar, and heading off for gigs with his fiddle tucked perilously under one arm.

'They were really good to me,' says Aly. 'They gave me money when I was broke – and I was broke a lot then, because I think I was earning about £2 a night playing in folk clubs, and I had left Shetland with nothing. All the money I had before I left Shetland I put in the bank for my return air fare. It was good to have that security, knowing I could get a flight back if things got bad.'

At the same time, Aly regarded his new colleagues with some degree of trepidation. 'They had been brought up in Glasgow, which was a hard city, and they knew how to take care of themselves. They could get pretty tough when they felt it was required.'

Aly had never seen any violence in Shetland – at least, not the 'casual' violence that Billy Connolly talks about later in this book – apart from the occasional Wild West brawl in Lerwick when a Norwegian or Swedish fisherman asked one of the local girls up for a dance. 'But if somebody came up to Billy and said something cheeky – *bang*! That was the end of the conversation.'

Musically, the spell with Billy and Tam did Aly nothing but good. He began to get a few more solo bookings as people with influence on the folk scene heard him, and Billy's commanding presence on stage helped him to build up his own confidence (although, in truth, Aly will always be nervous when he steps on to a platform, whether it be the Carnegie Hall in New York or the Carnegie Hall in Dunfermline).

Aly never became a fully-fledged member of the Humblebums. He never recorded with them, and later Gerry Rafferty was to step in to make up the classic threesome that became known far beyond Scotland. Aly always felt that Billy Connolly really wanted to be a musician rather than a comedian. 'But everybody maybe wants to be something that they're not, and the way the cards fell, his fame had to be in his humour.'

Aly was enjoying life, enjoying Billy and Tam, and enjoying Glasgow – 'a wonderful, wonderful city' – but he was barely earning enough to live on. The solo gigs in the folk clubs that did come his way were going down well, but many of the club organisers were still unwilling to gamble on a solo instrumentalist as their main attraction, and Arthur Argo was having a tough job digging up work. It was Argo – whether by design or accident, we'll never know – who, in late 1968, booked two relatively unknown soloists into the Green Tree pub in Dunfermline. The musicians in question had never heard of each other. Aly Bain, Shetland fiddler, was top of the bill – the organiser of the session just happened to be an amateur fiddle player, and knew where his priorities lay. The first set that night was taken by a spindly-framed bundle of human energy from Lauder, in the Scottish Borders, called Mike Whellans, who played guitar American-style and blew/sucked some mean blues harmonica. Aly had the solo spot at the end of the night, but he and Whellans had a drink during the interval and decided to get together for the finale. Mike Whellans remembers the occasion very well. 'It just took off,' he says. 'And that night when I heard him I knew that he had a very special talent.'

Whellans' musical speciality was blues and American bluegrass, an area in which he was actually far ahead of anyone playing in Britain at the time. He also had some Scots songs in his repertoire, and his expertise on guitar enabled him to be a fine accompanist to just about anything that was going on.

Argo, sitting in the audience as it erupted at the end of the session, must have smiled quietly to himself. The seemingly accidental coupling had fulfilled all his expectations. The musicians knew it themselves, and it didn't take much in the way of coercion from him to bring about the inevitable decision: Bain and Whellans would go on the road as Scotland's answer to England's fiddle-guitar duo of Dave Swarbrick and Martin Carthy, who had made an impact on folk clubs both south and north of the Border.

The Bain-Whellans partnership was, as Billy Connolly says, 'a marriage made in heaven'. Connolly goes on: 'Aly and Mike were just completely beautiful together. They understood each other so well.'

Aly's appearances with the Humblebums became more sporadic as he and Mike got down to the task of building a repertoire. It was a mixed bag of stuff: Scots fiddle tunes, American country and bluegrass songs and instrumentals, traditional Scots and contemporary songs sung by Whellans, harmonica blues, and, of course, Shetland reels, where the guitarist threw in swingy American-style runs that were the nearest thing to a typical Shetland accompaniment that Aly had found in Scotland.

By March 1969, the duo were ready for their first professional gig – in the unlikely setting of Earlston High School, in the Borders. Then they hit the road with a vengeance. Arthur Argo had contacted every folk venue in Britain, and Aly and Mike drove off in an unpredictable old mini-van to do a punishing round of one-night stands that had them working twenty-five days in the month.

'We were only getting something like £13 a night,' says Aly, 'so we had to do all these gigs to make the tour worthwhile. The van would keep breaking down and we would have to spend all our money fixing it. Lots of times we finished up sleeping on somebody's floor. Mostly, though, we stayed in awful bed-and-breakfast places – so awful that I've never stayed in one since. But it started to pay off. Apart from anything else, we were meeting all these people who heard us and wanted to book us for bigger gigs like concerts and festivals.

'After a while, it got to the point that you could throw a dart at a map of Britain, and we had almost certainly played there. We drove thousands and thousands of miles. But when you're twenty-three or twenty-four, it's all a big adventure, and you feel no pain.'

Argo took the duo down to the Keele festival, where London's musical press was gathered in force. They were suitably impressed. It was there that Aly first met the great Irish piper, Seamus Ennis. It was there, too, that he gave a quick fiddle lesson to a young man who was to make a name for himself with Steeleye Span – Peter Knight. Another English fiddler who got some tips from Aly that weekend was Barry

Dransfield, who had just taken up the instrument. Like so many of the big festivals, Keele generated tremendous spin-off in the form of more bookings for the Bain-Whellans duo. The Inverness Folk Festival of 1969 had a similar effect: most of the top attractions on the Scottish folk scene were there that year, including the Humblebums, the McCalmans, the Bitter Withy and Eddie and Finbar Furey. Aly and Mike were the new boys, and the audiences loved them.

As the months went on, Bain and Whellans became a much sought-after commodity in the folk clubs, if for no other reason than that the organisers knew they could depend on the versatile duo to offer a wide range of high-quality music and song that would guarantee something for just about everybody in the audience. Sara Grey, a fine American traditional singer and banjoist who was living at that time in Scotland, heard them in a folk club one night and immediately thought they should be heard in the States. She set about organising a huge American tour, and the boys flew off in October 1970 to begin an itinerary that made their British travels seem like a few gentle trundles to the seaside. There were forty-five gigs on that first tour, all one-night stands in the straggling network of coffee-houses that had spread out from Greenwich Village all down the east coast and into the Mid-West. It was a roller-coaster introduction to the United States, a country both Aly and Mike had long wanted to visit. They had little time to savour the delights of the New World as they desperately tried to pedal fast enough to keep to Sara's frantic schedule. It was all a bit

With Michael Cooney (left) and Dave Bromberg in Iowa City on the first American tour with Mike (1970). Aly describes it as 'probably the greatest experience of my life'

1/.

OCTOBER 1970   AMERICAN TOUR
TUES. 20TH — BINGHAMTON UNIVERSITY, OF NEW YORK,
WED. 21ST — CORNELL UNIVERSITY, ITHACA,
THURS. 22ND — SYRACUSE, UNIVERSITY, SYRACUSE.
FRID. 23RD — THE ARK, COFFEE HOUSE. ANN ARBOUR, MICHIGAN,
SAT. 24TH — THE ARK. COFFEE HOUSE. ANN ARBOUR. MICHIGAN.
SUN. 25TH — STONY BROOK UNIVERSITY, LONG ISLAND NY.
MON. 26TH — TRAVEL TO MONTREAL
TUES. 27TH — THE YELLOW DOOR COFFEE HOUSE, MONTREAL,
WED. 28TH — THE MOOSE HALL, COFFEE HOUSE, MONTREAL,
THURS. 29TH — THE YELLOW DOOR, COFFEE HOUSE, MONTREAL,
FRID. 30TH — THE YELLOW DOOR, COFFEE HOUSE, MONTREAL.
SAT 31ST — THE TRY WORKS COFFEE HOUSE, NEW BEDFORD, MASSACHUSETTS,

(OUR FIRST AMERICAN TOUR.)

2/.

NOVEMBER 1970   AMERICAN TOUR.
SUN, 1ST — BOSTON FOLKSONG SOCIETY, BOSTON,
MON, 2ND — TRAVEL TO CAMDEN MAINE,
TUES, 3RD — OFF.
WED, 4TH — THE UNIVERSITY OF MAINE,
THURS. 5TH — THE UNIVERSITY OF MAINE,
FRID. 6TH — MALBORO COLLEGE, VERMONT,
SAT. 7TH — PUTNEY SCHOOL, VERMONT
SUN, 8TH — IRISH CENTRE, PHILADELPHIA, AFTERNOON CONCERT, PHILADELPHIA FOLK SOCIETY, EVENING CONCERT,
MON 9TH — THE FOLKLORE CENTRE, NEW YORK CITY.
TUES 10TH — THE BALDWIN SCHOOL NEW JERSEY, AFTERNOON CONCERT,
TUES 10TH — DREW UNIVERSITY, MADISON NEW JERSEY, EVENING CONCERT
WED 11TH — HARVARD STREET, COFFEE HOUSE, BOSTON
THURS 12TH — OFF.
FRID 13TH — FOLKSONG SOCIETY, WASHINGTON.
SAT 14TH — FAMILY SING COFFEE HOUSE, POUGHKEEPSI
SUN 15TH — NORTHERN NEW JERSEY FOLK SOCIETY, EAST ORANGE, NEW JERSEY
MON 16TH — FLY TO IOWA CITY
TUES 17TH — UNIVERSITY OF IOWA
WED 18TH — GRENELL UNIVERSITY, IOWA.
THURS 19TH — FLY TO CHICAGO.
FRID 20TH — UNIVERSITY OF CHICAGO.
SAT 21ST. — OFF.
SUN 22ND — INDIAN NECK FOLKSONG SOCIETY, NEW HAVEN
MON 23RD — TRAVEL TO TORONTO,
TUES 24TH — FIDDLERS GREEN FOLK SOCIETY, TORONTO
WED 25TH — TRAVEL TO MALBORO, VERMONT,
THURS 26TH — CAFE LENA, SARATOGA,
FRID 27TH — CAFE LENA, SARATOGA,
SAT 28TH — CAFE LENA, SARATOGA,
SUN 29TH — CAFE LENA, SARATOGA,
MON 30TH — UNIVERSITY OF PENNSYLVANIA.

Hectic schedule for the 1970 tour, organised by Sara Grey

on the wild side, and wild oats were duly sown. There were parties. There were girls. Lovely, eager American girls. And while Mike, whose Scottish bride was waiting somewhat anxiously for him at home, was grimly sticking to his vow of chastity, Aly was finding himself – not for the first time, or the last – the centre of adoring female attention. For decades, this had been the kind of thing that happened to crooners and pop singers, but raunchy sex appeal on the traditional fiddle was definitely something new.

Mike Whellans, who now lives in Denmark and appears as a supercharged, blues-hustling soloist all around Europe, recalls that first American tour as being perhaps the craziest he has ever done, although he feels it served to sharpen the duo's individual capabilities and also weld them tighter together. And yet an indication that cracks were appearing on the surface of the music came when a review in the *New York Times* was headed: 'Bain and Whellans go their separate ways in concert.' It was, on the whole, a very favourable write-up, but the critic had clearly found some difficulty in figuring out just precisely what the duo were meant to represent musically, when

At the Buffs Club in 1969, when Aly first took Edinburgh by storm

Mike and Aly on their first trip abroad (1970). They played at the Tivoli in Copenhagen for a month – 'fun but hard work'. They got £6 each per night, but a beer cost £3

Session at the Inverness Folk Festival in 1970, when Aly and Mike topped the bill. Left to right: Martin Carthy, Davy Graham, Aly, Iain Mackintosh (partly hidden), Tam Harvey, Mike

Mike would follow a set of fiddle reels with a version of Muddy Waters' *Got My Mojo Working*.

Fair point, as they say. The days of the Bain-Whellans pairing operating as a fiddle-guitar duo were numbered, and they were soon to embark on bigger things. But for Mike Whellans, it had been 'a very special kind of time for me. It set me up for what I am doing now. Most of all, I just enjoyed playing with Aly. I had never really heard Scots fiddle music before, apart from Scottish country dance bands on the radio, and Aly was a revelation to me.'

They made one album, where, just to confuse the *New York Times* man further, they threw in a sizzling revamp of the jazz classic *Sweet Georgia Brown*.

Meanwhile, Aly had made a domestic move which he was never to regret. One day in 1969 he hitched a lift from Glasgow to Edinburgh to play a solo gig at the Buffs club in Albany Street – now long defunct. He stayed the night in Edinburgh, and he has stayed in the city ever since, never returning to live in Glasgow. Aly met up with the McCalmans (Ian McCalman, Derek Moffat and Hamish Bayne), a bearded, beery trio of powerful singers who believed in letting their hair down when they were off-stage, and he took up residence in their notorious flat at No. 47 Forrest Road – an address synonymous at the time with music-making, wild partying and liver-busting boozing. The house was just a few doors along from Sandy Bell's Bar, which was then the hub of the folk scene in Edinburgh, and after every music session in the bar the musicians would adjourn at closing time to the flat, taking half the customers with them. This, together with Hamish Bayne's attempts to play his trumpet in the wee sma' hours, did not exactly endear them to the neighbours, one of whom had a close encounter with a frying pan when he politely knocked on the door to complain about the noise. In fact, the din was coming from a party upstairs, and Aly and Hamish had been alone in the flat, arguing over who was to fry and eat the last egg – life at 47 Forrest Road was well below the poverty line. Hamish answered the door with frying pan in hand, listened to the man's protestations, and then could take no more: 'Do you realise that we haven't eaten for two days, and we have one fried egg between us? And you're complaining about *noise*! I'll give you noise. Take that!' The clang of tinny metal on human skull echoed down the stairway.

That outbreak of domestic violence apart, Aly found Edinburgh a remarkably peaceful place after his year in Glasgow. There were other attractions, not least Edinburgh's folk scene, which he felt was much more active and advanced than anything he had come across in the west of Scotland.

'At that time I had begun to understand that if any music is going to survive, it's got to be good enough. What was lacking on the folk scene in Glasgow was anybody who could play more than three chords on the guitar. Three chords were the norm – and in some clubs still are. The exception in Glasgow was Hamish Imlach, a wonderful blues guitar player, and I loved what he was doing.

'So I began to think that that would be my mission in life. If you're political when you're young, you've always got to have something to hang your hat on, something you believe in, otherwise there's no point in doing anything. When I was in Glasgow, that aspect bothered me because standards of playing weren't improving, and people seemed quite happy with the way things were.'

Glasgow still appealed to him as a political hotbed. 'I've always thought that Edinburgh was totally wishy-washy politically – it never had the same vibrancy of Glasgow. And I frankly didn't like the Edinburgh people at first. They didn't talk the way they did in Glasgow, and didn't make friends easily. But what I did find was a kind of close-knit cell of people who were really interested in the music.'

Among the friends he found was the Irish piper Finbar Furey, who was not only to influence Aly musically but also to be the decisive factor in Aly's decision to settle down in Edinburgh. The two men hit it off straight away, and Finbar spent hours and hours teaching Aly tune after tune and explaining the intricacies of Irish music. 'Finbar knew all the tunes I wanted to learn. In Shetland, I had heard records of Sean Maguire when I was only thirteen years old. He was a big influence on what I did, and I had learned his tunes, note for note, from the records. But I wanted to know more, and Finbar was my teacher. At that time, he was just the most amazing piper. I thought he was absolutely incredible – and I still do.'

After many a late-night session of pipes and fiddle, Finbar and Aly would unwind with a morning sauna, talking music most of the time. Finbar remembers in particular that the Shetlander knew little in those days of the Irish art of stressing certain notes to give a tune a real lift. 'Aly was very fast, and playing the notes was no trouble to him, but he wasn't really playing them with what you might call an Irish accent.'

Irish accents don't come much thicker than Finbar's, and Aly listened, understood, and absorbed. Finbar Furey also steered Aly in a direction which many young fiddlers fail to take until they are older – towards slow airs. Finbar recalls spending half the night on just one Irish air, *The Blackbird*, and refusing to let a weary Aly go to bed until he was producing the long, heartaching sounds that the piece demanded.

It wasn't all one-way traffic. Aly had much to show Finbar about Scottish and Shetland music. At the same time, Aly was always somewhat awed in the presence of the big Irishman, an extremely affable, garrulous character, but one who had been a boxer in his youth and who didn't suffer fools gladly. Many years later, the two met up again at the 1993 Shetland Folk Festival on a day when Aly had been plied with whiskies by well-meaning Shetland friends glad to see him home again. (It really is bad form to refuse a drink from a hospitable islander.) We were in the folk festival club in Lerwick, where the drinks were served in plastic cups. Finbar, a reformed spirits-drinker who now confines himself to pints of Guinness, feigned surprise and alarm at seeing his old pal in such a wobbly state. Just as Aly was reaching across the table for his next shot of the hard stuff, the Irishman grabbed his arm and said: 'Listen to me, Aly Bain. You don't need this drink. But I need you, and music needs you, and Scotland needs you, and Shetland needs you, and the world needs you. You don't need *this*.' Finbar then picked up the cup, threw the contents into a nearby bin and crumpled the cup in his fist. Aly looked so glum at this point that Finbar put his arm round him and said: 'Cheer up, Aly. If you want a whisky, I'll get you a whisky.' The large dram was duly brought to the table, and Aly again stretched an eager paw. He

Meeting up with his friends the Corries (1969), who did so much to popularise folk music.
Aly says: 'I wish I could find that jumper'

was too slow: Finbar was there before him. He picked up the cup and swallowed the whisky in one gulp. Aly this time was able to produce a bemused smile.

'You see,' said Finbar, 'how good it feels when you don't have whisky? Have some Guinness instead.'

'I hate Guinness,' said Aly. But Finbar held his pint to his lips and forced some of the treacly-looking booze down his throat.

'Promise me,' said the Irishman, 'that you won't have another drop of whisky, and then we can be friends again.' Aly mumbled some kind of pledge in his ear, and, true to his word, he didn't have another drop – that day.

While the two were in Edinburgh, Finbar's persuasive methods were strictly exercised not on alcoholic therapy but on Aly's music. Finbar eventually left Scotland to return to Ireland with his Scots wife, by which time Aly had made up his mind to make Edinburgh his permanent base. Aly was a regular visitor to Sandy Bell's bar, but he wasn't there for the beer. 'There was so much music going on in Sandy Bell's. All the touring musicians used to go there – the Dubliners, the Chieftains and so on. And people were really interested in the music. The Scotia Bar in Glasgow was fine, but it was almost like a private club and not exactly buzzing with instrumental music as Sandy Bell's was.'

He recalls his first visit to the bar: 'I walked in and saw Hamish Henderson standing on a table singing *Free Mandela* and thought: this is the place for me!'

Chapter Four

BOY OF THE LOUGH

The Boys of the Lough band can rightly trace its pedigree all the way back to 1967, when Robin Morton, a Belfast student, persuaded two fellow Irish musicians, Cathal McConnell and Tommy Gunn, to form an instrumental trio for a folk-club tour in Britain. Morton played concertina and bodhran and also sang traditional songs, while McConnell was at the time all-Ireland champion on flute and whistle. Gunn, from Co Fermanagh, was a fiddle player of an older generation. Morton and McConnell had already done some gigs as a duo, operating under the straightforward, if lumpy, title of Robin Morton and Cathal McConnell. When they tried to fit Robin Morton and Cathal McConnell and Tommy Gunn on to the posters, they realised that something crisper was required. The issue became more pressing when they were booked for a television appearance in Carlisle, and the producer indicated that he needed something snappy by way of a title. It was apparently Gunn who then came up with 'the Boys of the Lough', after the reel of that name which had long been associated with the playing of the great Irish fiddler Michael Coleman.

The tour, though successful enough, was a one-off event, and the trio broke up afterwards, leaving Morton and McConnell to carry on as an occasional duo. When Morton moved to Edinburgh in the late 1960s to do a PhD on the history of madness — no doubt to strengthen himself for the trials and tribulations of a life in music that his clairvoyant eye could see on the horizon — he arranged for Cathal to team up with him again for a number of folk-club tours in Scotland and England.

It was on one such tour, in 1968, that the two Irishmen ran into another young duo that they knew was beginning to cause something of a stir on the scene — Messrs Bain and Whellans, no less. The occasion was the Aberdeen Folk Festival, and although inevitably the two duos felt some degree of rivalry towards each other, there was a lot of mutual respect, too. Aly recalls loving the music he heard at that time from Morton and McConnell, while Cathal's memory is of 'a wee man, smaller than myself, with winkle-picker shoes' who could play the fiddle in a way he had never heard before outside Ireland.

Early Boys: Aly, Robin, Dave and Cathal

It wasn't until the following year, however, that the two duos were able to get together for an impromptu session and found that they had a lot in common musically. A public performance at a folk festival in Falkirk really settled the matter, and they began to get a few gigs as a quartet under the Boys of the Lough banner. What started as an occasional band slowly drifted into something infinitely bigger, and as the diary of engagements began to fill up it became clear that there was just about enough work to justify the band going full-time.

In 1971 the Boys of the Lough took to the road on the first of several lengthy tours of the British folk clubs, with Robin Morton at the organisational helm. The four-piece line-up, performing mainly traditional Irish and Scots instrumental music with a few songs from Morton, was something of a sensation in the clubs, although Aly does remember one early Scottish gig at Broughty Ferry when the band played to an audience of eleven people in a hall that could hold six hundred. But the *aficionados* who packed the folk clubs were enthralled, and word quickly got around. The bringing together of Aly Bain and Cathal McConnell, two musicians of undeniable virtuosity, proved to be a particularly inspiring move, with one sparking off the other. Their big solo spot on *The Mason's Apron*, where Aly would produce a dazzling set of variations, only to have Cathal popping up on tin whistle to try to out-dazzle him with some quicksilver fingerwork, was a show-stopper everywhere, and they also gelled beautifully in the ensembles. Whellans' propulsive guitar and Morton's bodhran created a bustling rhythmic foundation that helped to drive things along.

'We began to get loads of work,' says Aly, 'but it wasn't enough to keep four people on the road. We found that most of the folk clubs were only charging fifty pence at the door. After a while, we began to insist that we would only work in places that charged £1 – the average folk-club audience was about a hundred, so that meant £100 for us. But after we had paid for the hotel, transport and so on, it still left us with next to nothing.'

Some of the band were finding the going tough, but it wasn't for financial reasons that Mike Whellans decided to leave them in 1972. When he had been playing in the duo with Aly, he had had ample opportunity to do his own thing – whether hollering the *Stormy Monday* blues or imitating the sound of a train on the harmonica. With the Boys, however, he found himself locked into the role of rhythm guitarist, and while he loved the music and the offstage 'crack', he was itching to get out there on his own. They parted the best of friends, and a long-haired lad from Leith, Dick Gaughan, was drafted into the group. The picture of the band on the front cover of their first album had already been set up by the printers by this time, and they had to do a nifty job of masking out Mike Whellans and superimposing Dick Gaughan. (If you happen to have the album, take a look and see if you can spot the join.)

Gaughan was a major acquisition in that not only was he a fine player of traditional tunes on guitar but he was also in those days a towering, uninhibited singer of Scots ballads. He made every vibrant word throb with emotion and brought new life and meaning to the most ancient of lines – although sometimes, it has to be said, not all of the words came out distinctly, so ferociously did Gaughan deliver them in his broad Scots accent. At the same time, Cathal McConnell was beginning to assert himself as a singer with the band. Cathal favoured the sweet, pure style of his homeland, and the contrast of the two voices dealt the Boys a further winning card in their hand.

At this point, the band moved into a hectic spell of activity that was to pay handsome dividends in the future. Over in Boston, Wendy Lawrence, who had heard Aly playing with Mike in the States and been suitably impressed, was taking time out to set up an American tour for the Boys of the Lough. Nearer home, the band were recording their album for Bill Leader's Trailer label and doing the rounds of the summer folk festivals. The real turning point came just before the American tour, when they appeared at the 1972 Cambridge Folk Festival. The Cambridge festival had been running every year since the mid-'60s, taking its cue and its scale from the big American festivals. Within the marquees dotted around the Cambridge site, reputations were made and lost – at least, according to the London media people who attended the festival in droves.

The Boys found themselves on a bill which included some illustrious figures from the American folk scene – Arlo Guthrie, Steve Goodman, Kris Kristofferson, Loudon Wainwright III and Derrol Adams. The Dubliners, hugely popular at the time, were there. So, too, were England's Peter Bellamy, Ralph McTell and Jasper Carrot (many years later to become a household name in Britain as a television comedian).

It was a daunting gig for the Boys, but they rose magnificently to the occasion. As

With John Sheahan and Barry McKenna of the Dubliners at the Cambridge Folk Festival (1972)

The Boys of the Lough take a break during recording of the first album for Bill Leader in London (1972). Left to right: Dick Gaughan, Aly, Cathal McConnell and Robin Morton

The king: Jean Carignon

the influential *Melody Maker* critic, Andrew Means, recorded: 'The Boys nearly ran away with the festival. At one point late on Sunday night they had what seemed like half the main marquee tent on their feet dancing. It was nearly lift-off.'

Alongside a picture of the Boys in action, Means continued: 'Their music is so precise and accomplished that Aly Bain, Dick Gaughan, Robin Morton and Cathal McConnell are virtually the only people who can detect their own mistakes. That pathetic compère from *Monty Python* could have summed them up when he choked on his insufficient superlatives.'

The Boys may have quibbled when they first read Means' review – mistakes? what mistakes? – but there was no denying that this was heady stuff, eagerly read by just about everyone who mattered in the folk-music business.

It was at that festival that Aly renewed acquaintance with the American singer-songwriter Loudon Wainwright, who had heard him playing in the States with Mike Whellans. 'We had a few cocktails,' as Loudon puts it, 'and it turned out that Aly had lost his fiddle. He had laid it down somewhere, but he couldn't remember where. Aly was close to tears.' There began a drunken search through the sprawling Cambridge encampment – through, as Loudon recalls, 'the darkness, the mud, the sleeping bags, the bodies, the people milling about, the chaos'. They were joined by several members of the Dubliners, who gruffly offered Aly helpful reassurance: 'Whoever took your fiddle, my God we'll find the bastard and kill him.' The Dubliners, who had been warming to the self-allotted task in front of them, were quite put out when the fiddle finally turned up, tucked safely under the stage by some thoughtful folkie.

Mislaid fiddles apart, Cambridge '72 was a triumph for the Boys. 'We were bombarded with offers from agents and managers,' says Aly. 'People like Jo Lustig, who was a very powerful guy and could have got us just about any gig we wanted. But we said no, we would rather do it ourselves. When I look back, it was probably a mistake, but we'll never know.' To this day, the Boys are in sole control of their own affairs.

Suitably pysched-up by Cambridge, they set off a week or so later for their first American tour, and soon found themselves in the exciting natural amphitheatre of the Fox Hollow Festival in New York State. In terms of sheer size, this festival was not one of the majors, but it was an important showcase. Again, the Boys seized the opportunity to delight the two-thousand-strong crowd – and, of course, the folk-scene fixers – with the quality of their music. It was at Fox Hollow that Aly first met one of his great musical heroes, the brilliant French-Canadian fiddler Jean Carignon. Years later, he proudly presented Carignon as one of the stars of his *Down Home* television series.

It was at Fox Hollow, too, that Aly met a stunningly beautiful American girl, Lucy Ullman, who played the piano and loved folk music. Like the other performers, the Boys had been billeted in a tent. One morning, as Aly stumbled out of it, rubbing his eyes, he tripped over Lucy, who had parked herself there in the hope of catching his attention. 'I had made up my mind this man was going to be my husband,' she told me once.

Lucy caught his attention, all right. 'She looked like an Indian princess,' says Aly. There was an instant, magnetic rapport. Within a year, they were Mr and Mrs Bain.

That tour, too, the Boys played the famed Café Lena in Saratoga Springs – run, in Loudon Wainwright's words, 'by a larger than life, and larger than most people, woman called Lena Spencer'. For Aly, it was a return visit to this trendsetting coffee-house which had served as a proving ground for the likes of Joan Baez, Bob Dylan and the McGarrigle Sisters – he had been there in 1970 with Mike Whellans. Again, the Boys were a hit, although few of the coffee-house addicts, brought up on an almost total diet of singer-songwriters, had ever heard this kind of music before.

Loudon Wainwright remembers hearing Aly at Café Lena on the earlier tour with Whellans. Loudon was married at the time to Kate McGarrigle, whose knowledge of Irish and Scots music, and her enthusiasm for it, had got Loudon interested enough to go along to the gig. 'I remember being just knocked out by Aly's playing,' says Loudon. 'You could just tell that you were watching a virtuoso at work. I'll never forget that first sight of him, playing away with a cigarette hanging from his lips. Amazing. Plus, of course, I couldn't understand a word he said!

'Over the years, I got to know him better. He would come and visit when he was touring and we would go fishing and swimming together. I also have the distinction of being the only person – apart from the bride and groom – to have been at both of his weddings. Some months after the official ceremony at Ardsley in New York State, I

The Shetland wedding march (1973), filmed for BBC Television. Alex Pottinger has a shotgun to ward off the dreaded 'trows'. Best man Arthur Argo can just be glimpsed behind Lucy. Bringing up the rear are Aly's mum and dad and behind them is the late Donnie B. Macleod, television presenter, and the bearded Bill Hook, TV producer

Drinks all round after the Shetland wedding ceremony. Left to right: Arthur Argo, the groom, Loudon Wainwright III, the bride and Tom Anderson

happened to be touring in England and went up to Shetland for the ceremony there. I can't say I remember much about it, but I *do* remember having a very fine conversation with a Shetland pony at around 5 a.m.'

Incidentally, Loudon Wainwright, in answer to the daft-laddie question 'What's special about Aly Bain's playing?' with which I persistently prodded everyone I spoke to in the course of preparing this book, came up with an answer that perhaps only an American could have given: 'Like all great musicians, he *swings* – and *hard*. That's what it's all about – swinging, technique and feel.'

That first, relatively brief American trip by the Boys helped to set them up for a lifetime. In New Jersey, they were heard by Janet and Jules Schneider. Janet, a choreographer, was so enchanted with the music that she volunteered her services as the Boys' American agent and was soon setting up a much bigger tour for the following year. Janet went on to organise a six-week American tour every spring. 'The tours got bigger and bigger,' Aly says. 'Eventually they became too big for Janet to handle, because she had a young family to look after. So her husband took over. Being an accountant, with a razor-sharp brain, Jules soon had the band going all over the States for much bigger fees. If it hadn't been for people like Sara Grey, Wendy Lawrence and Janet and Jules, the band might never have got to where it is today.'

At the last count, the Boys had made no fewer than forty-two tours of the States – which averages out at roughly two per year. The US of A has been the great provider, but the Boys have paid their dues in terms of the consistently fine music they have delivered (one American writer hailed them as 'illustrious ambassadors from the Celtic world'), and the way in which they have opened the American door for countless other Irish and Scots bands.

Aly Bain feels strongly that the band started off with an ideal and it was the security of the American tours which enabled that ideal to be preserved rather than tarnished in any way. 'In the beginning, all we wanted was to get traditional music heard, and we were going to make sure it was heard, because it was good music. We were young then. We weren't doing it for money. We were doing it for other reasons, idealistic ones. But at the same time we had to make a living. Opening up America meant that we could actually make money without ever losing the ideal.'

And to all those people at home who bemoan the fact that the Boys spend so much of their time in the States, Aly has this to say:'We couldn't have made it in Britain as a band. I don't think we could have made it right through the '70s without America. It was America that in a way subsidised everything we did. We'd have this huge tour every spring, and out of that we made enough money – along with what we made here – to survive.'

Above all, the Boys played a pioneering role in introducing Celtic music to the American folk scene, where, with honourable exceptions like the singer Jean Redpath, Scots and Irish performers were virtually unknown. True, the Irish community clubs that are to be found all over the States had their singers and pipers, and they provided the first American platform for Dublin's Chieftains before they became a professional touring band. Scots music would emerge out of the shadows at the popular summer

Highland Games. But in terms of a committed folk audience, there was precious little happening before the Boys of the Lough began their triumphal procession through New York State and down the east coast in the early 1970s.

'They were amazed that we knew so much about their music,' says Aly, 'because they really didn't know much about ours. When the Boys went to America in the beginning, most of the people we played for had never heard our kind of music before, unless they were recent immigrants from Scotland or Ireland.'

During his most recent American tour, Aly found that a host of Celtic bands were working there at the same time – Altan, De Dannan, the Battlefield Band. 'What people don't always understand is that the Boys of the Lough started it all, created the market if you like. We weren't playing the Irish clubs. We were playing the coffee-house folk scene, which was very much an American thing. What they were listening to at the time was Bob Dylan and Joan Baez and a few old-timey American players like Jay Ungar, who was beginning to come through, and the New Lost City Ramblers, a group of young revivalists from New York.'

The pioneering work goes on, of course. Even today, as the Boys explore new territory in the States, they find themselves playing to audiences who have never heard Scots fiddle music before. At the same time, there has been a dramatic upsurge of interest in the past twenty years. When Aly was in San Francisco recently, everybody he met seemed to have an almost encyclopaedic knowledge of Irish music. 'They know every band, every player. That's how things have grown, and bands like Capercaillie are walking into a scene where people know what they're trying to do musically, but it's a scene that took years to build up.'

He has no grudges about other bands doing the business on the Boys' favourite patch. Every band is different, he argues, and the Boys are perhaps more different than others.

What was different in the early days, apart from the fresh Celtic breeze, was the fact that the Boys played in unison, with every instrument glued to the melody line. As Aly points out: 'In an American band, every instrument plays a different part. In a bluegrass band, they've got one fiddle on melody, one fiddle on harmony, mandolin on harmony and maybe voices as well singing in harmony. I think our first American audiences were knocked out at the idea of everybody basically playing the tune, which we were doing at that time. We didn't really have any accompaniment either, except for some guitar and Robin's bodhran, and because of that the fiddle, flute and concertina had to drive the music along. If you listen to the early tapes of the Boys of the Lough, we were all playing at tremendous speed. There was a hell of a drive. Without accompaniment, we would put in twice the effort to get over the melody side of it. And that was hard work.'

Hard work, yes, but fun as well. 'What we liked about the scene in America is that it wasn't built on the purist thing that we found in Britain. Everyone was in there because they enjoyed playing or listening to music, whether it was traditional or not. It was one big musical free-for-all.'

And it was that kind of open-eared attitude, of course, that enabled the Boys of the

Lough to do their own thing (paradoxically, just about as 'purist' a thing as could be found on either side of the Atlantic). They were accepted into the American folk fold with open arms – because it was abundantly clear to all who listened that this was great music, brilliantly played.

What helped, too, was the immense and very endearing American fascination with roots. Few Americans with British ancestry seem able to resist the magnetic pulse that eventually hauls them into the bank to pull out their savings and make the long and expensive journey to brood silently on the bare hills of some remote, windswept crofting settlement in the Western Isles of Scotland, where their great-great-grandmother might, and on the other hand might not, have been born.

In the 1970s, roots were big in the States. 'When they heard our music,' says Aly, 'they could see how it formed the basis of their own music, and they were intrigued by the connection.'

The time was right for Aly and the Boys in other ways. Acoustic music was already making a comeback – certainly among the middle-class college generation – as the high-decibel all-electric thunderers of the '60s began to lose their mind-numbing appeal. There was a growing hunger for real things – real food, real nature, real sounds. The shadow of the Vietnam War hung over the nation like an ugly vision in a bad dream, so protest was big, too – nowhere bigger than on the folk circuit.

Aly was acutely aware of the political buzz at the time, and reassured by it. 'The people who were organising the coffee-house scene were anti-war, anti-establishment. They were looking for new things and they were looking for support and new ideas. Then we came in. We thought the same way as they did. We were anti-war, anti-establishment – we were anti everything they were anti.'

In those days, one glance at the four members of the Boys of the Lough was sufficient to tell you that these guys were almost certainly not pillars of Rotary Club society who spent their Sunday afternoons weeding the begonia patch. Dick Gaughan, in particular, was going through a quite alarmingly unkempt, don't-give-a-damn phase, with long, straggly hair that looked as if it hadn't been washed for months. The band would come on stage with drinks and cigarettes, often wearing the same clothes that they had played in, and slept in, the previous night.

But their music, to American ears, was revolutionary, too, both in its commitment to the ideal of traditional roots and, of course, in its sheer newness. 'We just happened to go there at the right time,' says Aly, 'and our music fitted in exactly.'

That 1972 tour with the Boys gave Aly his first real chance to get to know a country that was to become, in a sense, his second home – a place he never tires of visiting. 'It's such a beautiful, big country, or more like twenty different countries. Apart from that, it has to be the most musical place in the world. In that respect, I feel very much at home when I'm there. People are completely open-minded about music. They don't put it in little boxes as we do. If it's good, it's okay. Ordinary people from all over the world brought their music and traditions to America, making it a melting-pot of cultures, so there are no musical barriers. America is a great platform for music. They have the climate for outdoor festivals, and during the summer there are hundreds of these, full of great musicians.'

At the same time, though, he has reservations about the political scene in the States, particularly the way in which the post-Vietnam years seemed to knock the stuffing out of the protest movement. Vietnam was, he feels, the turning point. 'After that, America seemed politically to go back to sleep. It's important to have a political opposition in any country, but that doesn't really exist in the States. There is no Left, just Right and further Right. One either succeeds the American way or not at all.'

One incident that brought home to Aly the sharp edge of the American dream was when he collapsed in acute pain at an airport on his way to Austin, Texas. An ambulance was summoned and he was rushed to the nearest hospital, only to be dumped outside on the steps because he didn't have a credit card. 'I lay there in agony for half an hour before the band's agent arrived with a card, and they agreed to take me in. They found I had a stone on my kidney and they treated me. But God knows what would have happened to me if I had been dying and there had been no one with a credit card. The hospital was called the Baptist Memorial Hospital. Well, they certainly gave me something to remember: I couldn't help thinking at the time of how Bessie Smith had bled to death because none of the hospitals would let her through the door.'

As well as Fox Hollow, the Boys took in a much larger 1972 festival at Philadelphia, where the crowd was nearer 10,000, and they got a Cambridge-like

The Boys of the Lough played the Border Festival in El Paso many times and were made honorary citizens in 1981 along with D.L. Meynard. It was one of many such honours throughout the United States

reception. Even *Rolling Stone*, that cool chronicler of the hip scene, took note: '. . . and a quartet of young British instrumentalists-singers, the Boys of the Lough, set the Saturday night crowd howling and dancing in the full fury of an August thunderstorm with Gaelic tunes played on fiddle, guitar and bodhran.' Poor Cathal's efforts on flute and whistle didn't apparently merit a mention.

The Boys of the Lough were the first British band of their type to get visas that allowed them to work in the States. 'You had to prove to the American authorities that you weren't taking work away from American musicians,' says Aly. 'So we had to prove to them that we were playing music that they couldn't play.' Confronted with an eloquent plea from Kenny Goldstein, who was professor of folklore at Philadelphia, the immigration people quickly realised that they couldn't win this one and issued the documents.

That was an important breakthrough, because after their appearance at the Philadelphia festival, the offers began to pour in and there was clearly enough work to justify Janet Schneider in setting up a major American tour for the following year.

In the event, the band made not one tour but two in 1973. This time, though, they had a new Boy with them. Dick Gaughan, like Whellans before him, had set his mind on a solo career and decided to leave. Aly was dismayed at the news, as Dick's Scottish input into the music, besides being of the highest calibre, had meant that the Boys' repertoire had struck a nice balance between Scots and Irish material. But there was no changing Dick's mind: he was going.

On their British tours, Aly and Mike Whellans had got to know Dave Richardson, a university student living in Durham, whose spare time was occupied in playing concertina, banjo and mandolin, plus perfecting a bouzouki-like instrument that he had built with the help of Stefan Sobell and christened 'the bazouki'. With a first-class honours degree in molecular biology under his belt, he was working on a post-graduate certificate of education 'in the hope that it would buy me time to finish my PhD'. He never did complete the thesis. The Boys put paid to that. Their offer to him of a three-week American tour seemed harmless enough at the time. 'We had found ourselves unexpectedly a man short,' Aly recalls, 'and we asked Dave to fill in just for that tour until we could get someone fixed up permanently.'

But it was Dave who became the permanent fixture, and although he returned briefly to his studies after that tour, he has been with the band ever since. Aly reckons that Dave 'got bitten by the bug' after touring with the Boys in the States 'and realised that our kind of life was a damned sight more interesting than being in a laboratory for the rest of his days, cutting up frogs and things'.

Dave was arguably the man with most to lose by joining the band, although Robin Morton had established the precedent of a highly qualified academic throwing it all up for folk music. Fortunately, I can report that Dave has no regrets to this day. After Robin Morton's departure in 1979, Dave inherited from him the unenviable task of running the band's affairs. He took to it like the proverbial duck to water and now runs a highly efficient organisation from his house in Edinburgh, handling all the band's concert, recording and television bookings, setting up the travel itineraries and so on.

'We've even got,' he says proudly, 'a fax machine.'

Dave Richardson acquitted himself so well on the 1973 tour that he won his place on musical grounds alone. The extra instruments that he brought into the band helped to give the sound a new, denser texture that proved popular with the fans and the critics. A measure of how quickly things were developing for the Boys at that time can be taken from the 'New Year's Honours List' for '73 compiled by *Folk Review*, which awarded them an accolade 'for the most meteoric rise' of the year. Their first album, entitled simply *The Boys of the Lough* (Trailer LER 2086), had much to do with this. Michael Grosvenor Myer, whose defiantly unfolky name did not prevent him from becoming one of *Folk Review*'s most authoritative writers, commented: 'This record will help to explain why the Boys are currently one of the most respected line-ups on the scene, and probably the biggest draw in the clubs.'

The album was also picked by *Melody Maker* as folk record of the month (May 1973): 'The group is one of the most encouraging and talented units to emerge through the revival.' And I seem to recall that a chap called Alastair Clark also gave the album an enthusiastic welcome in *The Scotsman*. Clearly, in addition to their American conquests, the Boys had been making a major impact on home territory.

Altogether, it was an exciting year for the band and especially for Aly, who managed to find time for his wedding in the States and the subsequent televised ceremony in Shetland, where his old guru, Tom Anderson, proudly led the way as the Forty Fiddlers — or at least as many as could be rounded up for the occasion — strode along the country road with the smiling couple following behind. What the TV cameras couldn't show was the king-size hangovers which afflicted just about everybody involved, after the traditional pre-nuptial celebration the night before.

That year, too, saw the beginning of a significant shift in the Boys' professional approach. Riding on the unanticipated wave of popularity, they signed up for a concert in the prestigious Royal Festival Hall in London, fearing an almighty flop. In fact, they played to a packed auditorium. It served to reinforce the growing view that their future lay in bigger venues than the faithful but essentially makeshift folk clubs could ever hope to offer.

By the following year, the Boys' London agents, Jean Oglesby and Jane Winder, were actually putting it in writing in a press hand-out which reached me at *The Scotsman*: 'During September, the Boys of the Lough completed their final tour of the folk clubs, as they will now be concentrating entirely on concert tours both here and abroad. They return, at the end of November, from their fifth tour of America.'

It went on to announce a Scottish and English concert tour in which the Boys would feature two guest performers, the Gaelic singer Flora McNeill and the clarsach player Alison Kinnaird (Robin Morton's wife). The ladies almost stole the show. My review in *The Scotsman* gave them due credit: 'Altogether, it was a great night for traditional music. Alison Kinnaird got a huge cheer for her exquisite solos on the clarsach, the small harp of Irish-Scots lineage. And to cap it all, there was the superbly expressive Gaelic singing of Flora McNeill, whose love songs and waulking songs were so melodic and rhythmical that I for one hardly noticed that they were in a tongue I could not understand.'

In choosing Flora and Alison, the Boys were underlining their commitment to traditional music. At the same time, they were implicitly indicating that they didn't feel quite ready to tackle a full concert entirely on their own. That was to come later.

The process of the Boys' graduation from folk scene to concert hall had already begun in the States by this time. So many people wanted to hear the band that the coffee-houses, with a capacity audience of perhaps eighty or even less, simply couldn't cope. Besides, the coffee-house circuit, like the folk clubs in Britain, could not support the costs of keeping a professional band on the road, unless the musicians were prepared to flog themselves round the venues and burn themselves out in pursuit of a living wage. In strict financial terms – although the goodwill gained was worth a small fortune – the early American tours came into the category of what businessmen would call loss-leaders, with little or no cash in the bag at the end of a long, tiring schedule.

Aly and the Boys didn't taste 'real money' until they gently moved away from the smoke-filled rooms of the folk scene to enter the stage doors of the less predictable, often slippery, open arenas frequented by the great American public.

Let's be clear about this change of strategy, because the folk scene is never short of people who are suspicious of success, and there will always be mutterings of 'sell-out' when a folk band starts reaching a wider audience. The only selling out was done at the box office. The music that the Boys played was not compromised in any way. They carried on playing and singing precisely as they had done before. They may have smartened themselves up a bit, trimmed the lanky locks and beards, put on a clean shirt and left their beer cans and fags in the dressing-room, but that was the sum total of the adjustment. There was no slick video to feed to the television stations, no gimmicky 'single' to aim at the pop charts, no attempt to build up a repertoire of quasi-Clancy Brothers chorus songs that would open up the lucrative goldmine of audience participation, no gorgeous Gaelic girl to whisper into the microphone. Perhaps most remarkable of all, there was no movement on stage at all, apart from the feet tapping on the boards and the busy elbows and fingers flying: the Boys sat, as they always had done, on four wooden chairs, much in the way that a classical string quartet would do, and didn't even stand up for their solo spots.

As Aly emphasises: 'We were pushing the music in a purist kind of way. We just wanted to preserve it and play it right. There were plenty of people playing all the other stuff, so we never felt a need to go in that direction. This was going to be our music, and we wanted as many people as possible to come out and hear it.'

The first American concert tours were concentrated on the university campuses, where there was not only a lot of interest in traditional music but also the money to pay for it in the form of entertainment budgets that were often founded on some wealthy benefactor's endowment. And, of course, the college circuit wasn't just confined to the east coast, where the Boys had made their early mark. During the '70s the band began to move into the mid-west and by the end of the decade they had built up a big following on the west coast as well. It was to be some years, though, before they ventured into the southern states. 'There weren't many people organising things in the south,' says Aly. 'And while they had plenty of music, it was mainly country music and bluegrass, and it was a closed scene to us at the time.'

As soon as the financial position began to improve, the Boys took the wise decision to improve their lifestyle as well. Out went the stifling camper van. No longer would each man have to beg for a friendly floor to sleep on after the gig (assuming, of course, that a friendly young lady hadn't offered something more comfortable). They adopted the policy – and it's still adhered to – that if the Boys were going to live on the road, they were going to live well on the road. So, quite early in the Boys' career, they began booking good hotels in each town or city, even if it meant burning a sizeable hole in the profits. 'We started to look at how we could travel in more comfort,' says Aly, 'and how to space our tours out. We realised that touring wasn't a joke. If we were going to work in a professional way, then we had to arrive at gigs feeling fresh, and then the music would be fresh, too.'

The system wouldn't have been possible if the Boys had been at the beck and call of an independent tour promoter, who would naturally have attempted to squeeze as many gigs into the schedule as time allowed. The band did use the services of agents in the States, notably Janet Schneider, but because they were themselves the promoters they were able to dictate the logistics and the lifestyle. Aly points out: 'We had control over how many nights off we had, how many nights we worked, and where we stayed. We also insisted on going out to good restaurants to eat good food. And we made sure that there would always be two or three days off in the middle of the tour when we could find some place to have a rest in the sun. That's still the case today. We look for comfort – as near the kind of comfort you could find in your own house. And if that means staying in five-star hotels, then we stay in five-star hotels, even though it's a strain financially. It was this that kept the band's sanity over the years, and kept us together.'

Early on, too, the band learned that no matter how tempting the offers might be, every night cannot be party night. The trouble with having friends in every corner of America is that they expect some fun when the Boys of the Lough are in town. Perhaps they remember the way the Boys were on the first couple of tours – innocents at large in the big, welcoming country, game for a laugh, game for anything. So barbecues are prepared. The booze is bought. But if the Boys have a plane to catch early next morning – thanks, but no. If there's no travelling or no gig next day, that's a different matter, and the Boys will be boys all over again.

'It used to be so wild,' says Aly. 'Nowadays, as on the last tour, there's maybe just the one party. Maybe it's something to do with our American friends getting older. They've got families now and responsibilities – just as we have – that they didn't have in the early days. And anyway, America has never been a big party scene like Scotland is or Ireland is. People there don't really drink much, and they don't smoke either – you are sent out on the balcony to smoke a cigarette, even in the winter. Mind you, I get more fresh air that way.'

'The quieter scene suits us fine. We can't handle parties when we're on tour. We might have a beer after the concert, but that's it. The pattern is that we're getting up at eight in the morning, catching a plane at nine and flying till lunchtime. We go to the

With Janet Schneider, the Boys' first American agent, at her New Jersey home

hotel, go to bed for a couple of hours, and the sound-check's at five. The concert's at eight, and it's eleven o'clock before it's over – and we're flying the next morning at eight . . . and so on.

'When we were playing the coffee-houses there was a party just about every night. But the concert situation is quite different. For a start, you don't meet the audience. They just come to the concert, listen to the music, and go home. Even if a lot of people come to the dressing-room, it's really just to say a few words before they leave.'

To be sure, Aly, who is a very gregarious fellow, does confess to missing that kind of people-contact, but he feels that the contact is still there in the relationship that the Boys are able to build with the audience. It's one of the secrets of their success: making friends with the rows and rows of unknown faces out there in the darkness.

In their wanderings across the United States, the band didn't reach the west coast until 1976, when they produced a triumphal performance at the San Diego festival in California. That festival opened up a lot of new doors. Later, they played the famous Bread and Roses festival in Berkeley, California, organised by Mimi Farina for an organisation which broadcast music into prisons. It was a star-studded cast at Berkeley – Pete Seeger, Arlo Guthrie, Mickey Newbury, Joan Baez, Buffy Saint-Marie, Tom Paxton, Rambling Jack Elliott, Maria Muldaur, Richie Havens . . . you name 'em, they were there. Yet again, the Boys excelled themselves and the 9,000-strong audience in the Greek Theatre went wild. 'They had never heard our kind of music before,' Aly recalls. 'We were the first Celtic band on the west coast. We played things

At the Navato Festival in California (c.1977) with Jules Schneider, Dewy Balfa and Rodney Balfa

like *The Mason's Apron* and brought the house down — we got about three encores, I think. The next night we had a solo concert in the Great American Music Hall in San Francisco, and were amazed to find that we had sold every ticket. We could hardly move in the dressing-room for managers wanting to sign us up.'

Celtic music had gone west with a bang, and California has been a happy stamping-ground for the Boys ever since.

It was on that first trip west that Aly had a blazing row with Arlo Guthrie, son of the famous Woody. Influenced no doubt by Bob Dylan's much-publicised conversion to Catholicism, some of the American folkies had gone the same way, much to Aly's horror. Arlo, too, was dabbling in religion, and Aly was determined to talk him out of it.

'How could you do such a thing?' said Aly. 'Your father fought the establishment and championed the poor all his life. What would he think? How can anybody get into religion after the revolution of the '60s?'

The situation became so heated that someone had to step in to pull the two men apart. Aly has always loved a good ding-dong of an argument, but in those days he was a lot more headstrong than he is now. No matter how distinguished the opposition might be, he would wade in with his terrier-like growls, fearless of the dangers. Even the gentle, pacific Pete Seeger came in for a Bain tongue-lashing as he and Aly sampled the joys of a jacuzzi on that same trip. The festival had laid on a lovely masseuse to keep the performers in good shape, and Aly and Seeger were having their toes softly massaged. All was peace, contentment, the good life. The two men had a mutual friend in Arthur Argo, and chatted away amiably about him and about Scotland. But the talk soon turned, as most Aly Bain conversations did at the time, to politics and eventually to communism. Pete Seeger listened carefully to what Aly had to say and then came up with: 'You know, Aly, the greatest communist of all was Jesus Christ.' Aly blew his top. Here was the father figure of the American folk revival, the great left-wing communicator to the people, the white champion of the underprivileged blacks, the brave victor over the witch-hunting congressional committees, seeming to go soft on religion. It was too much. Aly, in classic massage-parlour style, made an excuse and left.

It all seemed to fit in with Aly's assessment of the American political mind as being a bit on the naïve side. 'Most Americans didn't really understand what the Left was. They were correct in protesting about the Vietnam War, and Seeger was involved in that protest as well as the racial one, and that was wonderful. But it was all very shallow, and when the war ended, it all collapsed. And to cap it all, their generation finished up by voting for Reagan, just as ours had done for Thatcher.'

Americans reading this will no doubt see Aly's words as a sweeping generality, which, of course, they are. Some may even take the view that he is gnawing the generous hand that feeds him and should perhaps be wagging his tail instead. But Aly's political ideas are founded on the concept of equality – the kind of equality that really did exist in the uncomplicated, unblemished, time-warp world of his childhood years in Shetland, where every single inhabitant had stature and commanded respect, where people pulled together to help the unfortunates, where there were precious few fortune-builders and no tycoons, only relative degrees of poverty. Aly went from this to the richest country on earth, was uplifted to find revolution blowin' in the wind, and then saw it all slide back into the political doldrums. For music-lovers, there was one big bonus. It strengthened Aly's belief in the importance of music and culture, and his playing, which had always been a barometer of his mood, became more emotionally charged, more beautiful, more loving, as if he was saying: people who care are the ones that count.

And while politically the United States may no longer have counted for much, there was no doubting the power of the revival of acoustic music all over that huge country, a revival which was to go on and on. At the same time, the new American mood of environmental concern – amusingly if sardonically portrayed in the tee-shirt slogan which said: 'Gay whales against racism' – went hand in hand with the nurturing of traditional music. Americans cared all right. And the fact that they have cared about his music has been an inspiration for Aly over the years.

Between 1972 and 1978, the Boys of the Lough had thirteen tours of the United States, but they were also in demand at home, and during that time they recorded a string of albums, including *Second Album* for Trailer in 1974 and then *Recorded Live*, the first of several for Transatlantic Records. That was followed by *Lochaber No More*, with a stronger Scots accent than usual, and *The Piper's Broken Finger*. These albums appeared in the States on the Philo label, as did *Good Friends – Good Music*, where guest musicians were brought into the studio.

They also made their first forays into Europe, which, again, was largely virgin territory in terms of instrumental music, although Scots and Irish singing groups and soloists had been popular since the 1960s. Instrumentally, one or two electric-folk bands from England had made an impact, and on the acoustic side Finbar Furey and his brother Eddie had led the way and were building up a following in the folk clubs. The Boys at first tested the club circuit, but found it unedifying, perhaps because the all-singing, all-joking folkies who had gone before them had given the continentals an expectation of folk music as consisting essentially of chorus songs, hand-clapping tunes and a laugh a minute. The Boys soon abandoned the clubs for the European folk-festival scene, where there was at least the prospect of a listening audience. 'I found it very difficult to work in the clubs in Germany and Holland particularly,' says Aly, 'because I found there wasn't any real feeling for what we did. What they really seemed to like was stamping their feet and drinking beer.' Not all Scottish performers were so disenchanted; some have spent their whole careers with such audiences.

France and Spain were different, though, because there was already a strong indigenous musical tradition in those countries: 'We loved playing in France and Spain – we still do – and in the Scandinavian countries like Norway and Sweden, where there was a lot of fiddle playing. These countries were all rich in their own cultures, whereas Germany and Holland had come to rely almost entirely on imported music. The Germans had their music before the war, but Hitler used it in such a way that it became unfashionable later, so the Germans adopted Irish music.'

The big German market was theirs for the taking, but Aly and the Boys have never been in the business of performing anywhere so long as the dough is good. 'A lot of musicians made a lot of money out of Germany. Personally, I found it really soul-destroying. In America we found that there was a genuine appreciation of what we were doing, and we could play our music without ever feeling that we had to ram it down their throats.'

On one occasion, when they were in West Berlin, they unintentionally strayed into East Germany, which was then, of course, firmly isolated behind the Iron Curtain. As they drove further and further, the buildings became more decrepit and the cars fewer and fewer, and they realised that they had made a terrible mistake. They had visions of being arrested as spies – don't laugh, it happened in those days – and being incarcerated in a communist cell, where they would play to a captive audience for the rest of their days.

Finally they managed to steer their way back to the border, where an East German officer waved the car down and approached menacingly. When he found that the Boys were not only from Ireland and Scotland but also folk musicians, he welcomed them as long-lost buddies. As Aly puts it: 'He saw the Irish and Scots as being anti-establishment. He believed we were the minority fighting against a bigger enemy. Maybe he was right.' Delighted with the gift of some Boys of the Lough tapes, the officer opened the gates back to freedom.

Years later, Aly returned to East Germany. This time the visit was official – to play with the Boys at a big folk festival. They flew in on a rickety East German airliner

*Different angle: with Robin Morton during the
band's first trip to Bermuda (1978), when Aly put
his Shetland fishing skills to good use*

which still had wooden seats and wooden arm rests. For Aly, terrified of flying at the time, it was a nightmare flight. The festival was good fun, however, and Aly heard music he had never heard before, as the guest-list was almost entirely made up of performers from communist countries like Yugoslavia and Cuba who had never reached the West. The money was good, too – the equivalent of £500 per man per day. The problem was that it came in East German currency, which was worthless outside the country. The solution was to transform the cash into goods which they could take home, so they stuffed their jackets full of notes on the last day of the festival and went shopping. 'Dave bought an accordion,' Aly recalls, 'and I went looking for fiddles, but couldn't find anything. In fact, I couldn't find very much at all, as East Germany was a very deprived country. So I bought two coffee-grinders, six watches and a couple of cameras, but everything was very cheap, and try as I might I just couldn't get rid of the money.'

Exhausted with the shopping spree, they all went back to the hotel with about half of the money still in their pockets. They discovered that the Cuban band were having a farewell party. Problem solved. Aly recalls: 'We went out and bought cases of

Two great friends. Al Macenny (left), the Boys' driver and sound technician in the US for many years, with the late Jim Ringer

Aly, Tom and Willie at the Mariposa Folk Festival (1978)

champagne for the Cubans, who were great guys and they played great music. They gave us huge Havana cigars, and at the end of it all we handed them all the East German money we had left as well. It was some night.'

The '70s saw the Boys exploring new territory much nearer home – in the vast, beautiful terrain of the Highlands and Islands of Scotland, which had been left untouched by the urban folk bands. There was indigenous music there, to be sure, in the form of accordions, fiddles, pipes and, above all, Scottish country dance bands, which provided weekend entertainment in the village halls and at just about every social function. But concerts of any kind were a distinct rarity, and when the Boys of the Lough went off on a Highland tour in the mid-1970s that took them as far as the Hebridean isles off the west coast, they found themselves, not for the first time, in the role of musical trail-blazers.

'We started doing tours in the Highlands when nobody from the folk scene was doing it,' says Aly. 'We put up a few posters, placed a few advertisements in the papers and booked halls in places like Stornoway [Isle of Lewis] and Portree [Isle of Skye]. Lots of people came to see us, but they looked at us almost in a suspicious way at first, because this wasn't the kind of music they were accustomed to, although they could see the connection it had with their accordions, fiddles and pipes.'

The suspicious appraisal didn't last long. The Highlanders and Islanders soon took the Boys to their hearts, and the annual tour, while never in any way a money-spinner, became one that the band always looked forward to, with its packed little village halls and its splendid post-concert hospitality. 'There was a gap in their music, and I think we filled it,' says Aly, who feels that the Boys also helped to clear the ground for the instrumental revival in the Highlands. 'We provided a good reason, if you like, for learning an instrument, and all these young people started playing. Every year we went to the Highlands we could see more and more interest, more and more musicians.'

But it wasn't all band work for Aly in the '70s, for it was then that he began branching out a bit on his own when the Boys were off the road. While Dick Gaughan was with the band, for example, Aly teamed up with him for some duo gigs in the folk clubs. There was another fiddle tour with Tom Anderson in 1975. The seeds of what was to become a flourishing solo career, quite distinct from that of the band, were being sown.

Another lucrative, if less artistically rewarding, sideline that opened up in the early 1970s was the business of guest appearances on other people's albums. The first major performer to haul Aly into the recording studio was his fellow Scot, Bert Jansch, of the Pentangle. Dick Gaughan was on that session, too, around 1973, and they found themselves playing alongside not only the Pentangle's jazzy bass man, Danny Thompson, but also the brilliant American jazz drummer Dannie Richmond, long associated with the great Charlie Mingus. 'He was a genius,' says Aly, 'I'd never heard anything like this before.' To illustrate a piece of percussion that he had in mind, Jansch put on a track featuring the Fairport Convention drummer, Dave Mattacks, who was never what you might call a silky swinger. Richmond burst out laughing.

Aly, Dave and Tich with The Slowest Gun in the West Highlands (Ardrisaig, Scotland, 1979)

'What is that shit?' he said. Jansch wisely decided to let Richmond do his own spectacular thing. The album, *Moonshine*, didn't do particularly well, perhaps because Warner Brothers soon afterwards discontinued the label it was issued on.

On their last night in London, Jansch took Aly and Dick out on the town. It was a long, hard-drinking round of Jansch's favourite clubs and pubs. Bert was fond of his bevvy in those days, and he set a formidable pace. But Aly and Dick had to be at Fort William, in the north-west of Scotland, for a gig on the following night, so, much the worse for wear, they bade farewell to Jansch in the wee small hours and set off in the car from London. It was dawn when they reached Carlisle, in the north of England. At Glasgow, they snatched an hour's sleep and then headed off for the Highlands.

In a state of near-collapse, they finally reached Fort William. The man who was organising the gig was surprised to see them. 'Didn't you get the message that the gig is cancelled?' he said. The faces of the two dishevelled musicians went suddenly even paler than they had been before. Dick Gaughan, at the best of times, looked dangerous. Now he wore the icy expression of a man who shoots off your knee-cap for kicks. The promoter, who had a fine sense of self-preservation, was not about to make the newspaper headlines. He pulled out his wallet and handed over the money that he would have paid them if the gig had gone on.

Not long afterwards, Aly got a call from the former Fairport Convention singer and guitarist, Richard Thompson, who wanted him to appear with his wife Linda on their new album, *Hokey Pokey*. Thompson put the fiddler quite off his stride by arriving at the session in London and promptly going down on the studio floor to bow to Mecca — eastern religion and mythology were very much in vogue at the time. Aly's name featured prominently on the front cover of the record when it was issued in 1974, but in fact he is hardly heard, and he was forever puzzled by the whole exercise: 'They flew me all the way down to London to play four notes in B-flat that any fiddler could have played.'

Nevertheless, he found Thompson to be an inspiring musical collaborator. 'He has a fascination with Scots music — strathspeys and reels and things — I think because he was born in Scotland and left the country when he was a few months old. He must have liked my playing, because he used me on a lot of his records. I loved doing those albums. He's fantastic, a gifted musician and really inventive. He should be a huge star, and I don't know why he isn't. He's one of those musicians who seem to live perpetually on the edge of being mega-popular. After that first session, he always gave me something interesting to do. I could see what he was getting at musically — he's very emotional, like me — and we worked really well together. He has a great gift. I wish there were more like him.'

The one problem that Aly has found on recording sessions is that he is invariably expected to read his part. Aly's ability to read music is limited. He can work his way through a piece of sheet music, finding the notes and then stringing them together by ear once he has learned them. But even on folk recordings, the stars tended to hand him a scribbled score and expect him to come in on the count of four. Aly didn't like doing it that way, and began to insist that he listen to a recording of the tune before he played it. He would wander round the studio with a Sony Walkman plugged into his ears, listening to the music over and over again until it had sunk in. 'Then when the recording started I would invent something of my own instead of playing what had been written for me. It usually worked out better that way.'

Aly's first, and possibly his last, appearance on a rock record came in the 1980s when he and Phil Cunningham were asked by the Scots singer Fish, of Marillion fame, to supply a bit of Scottish music for one of the tracks on his new solo album. Phil, who, as well as being an ace accordionist and keyboard player, is a dab hand at composition, dreamed up a delightfully tricky little tune on the spot, and he and Aly rehearsed it until it was ready for recording. Fish's producer, a Londoner, listened to the finished piece and came over to the two musicians, who were feeling quite pleased with themselves. 'It's nice,' said the producer. 'Don't get me wrong, boys, it's nice. Like, you know, *really* nice. But it is a bit *busy*, isn't it?'

What he meant, of course, that it was far too clever: this was, after all, a rock record. Under protest, Aly and Phil put together some simple Scottish musical clichés, and the producer was overjoyed with their contribution. 'I found that scene really bizarre,' says Aly. 'I play music for music's sake – it has to mean something. But here I was supposed to add flavour to what the producer had in mind, and what he had in mind wasn't what I had in mind. We discovered then that rock records are mostly controlled not by the musicians but by the producers. I never allowed myself to fall into that trap again.

'I think hell to me is a bit like Miles Davis having to play *Wear a Yellow Ribbon* for eternity. Playing what other people want you to play is like becoming a computer. A conductor to me is like a boss telling you what to do – dig this, or shovel that. I couldn't take orders when it comes to music. It has to belong to you. It has to be your statement, your expression of life. Conductors and record producers to me are like politicians: they love power, but few of them do the things you feel need to be done.'

Rock recording studios are one thing. Rock festivals are a different matter. Here, it's the music that counts, and ever since the Boys of the Lough played at the huge, open-air Lincoln Festival in the mid-1970s, Aly has been happy to accept what he calls 'the Celtic novelty spot', secure in the knowledge that audiences, no matter how rock-orientated, invariably respond well to his music. Lincoln was the band's first appearance at one of these mammoth celebrations. The Beach Boys and Bob Dylan were the top attractions, and something like a quarter of a million people had come to hear them.

'We were absolutely at the bottom of the bill, in very tiny letters,' Aly recalls. 'So they put us into the worst possible slot – at ten o'clock in the morning. We went on to this huge stage. It had a sound system that was like two skyscrapers on either side of the band. As we looked out, we could see just two or three people ambling around. It was like a vast medieval encampment, with rows and rows of tents as far as the eye could see. It was like an army asleep. And then Robin went up to a microphone and tapped his bodhran to check the amplification. It was as if the heavens had opened. The noise boomed across the field, and all these long-haired people started crawling out of their little tents, with joints in their mouths, tripping over each other, to see what the hell was going on. They all sort of staggered towards the stage, and then they started dancing and flying about, and it was a great feeling. It was almost like being a pop star for a day. You got the impression of the kind of power these people feel when they're up there on stage, although it's a completely impersonal power – the volume takes over from the music.'

Aly was, in his own word, 'petrified' when he went on stage, but, as luck would have it, the first person who caught his eye in the crowd below was an old mate of his from Shetland. That settled him down, and one of the people who were impressed by his fiddling that morning was Spencer Davies, who had led one of Britain's top rock outfits, featuring Stevie Winwood, in the '60s and was now attempting to make a comeback with a new group. Davies took Aly for a drink and persuaded him that it would be a great idea if Aly came up on stage and played with him that night. Aly, buoyed up by a successful morning's business, readily agreed. Not for the first time, however, he made the mistake of overstaying his welcome in the hospitality tent, and it was dark by the time he got out, countless whiskies later. He settled under a tree to sleep it off. Aly woke up to find that it was raining, and his name was being called over the huge speakers. At first he thought he was dreaming. Then, remembering his date with Spencer Davies, he grabbed his fiddle and somehow found his way to the stage. There was no time for pleasantries, and Davies kicked the band off into a racing, roaring blues in E-flat, a key which is notoriously difficult on the fiddle. Aly was comprehensively lost. When Davies and the other musicians all turned to him, he realised that it was his turn to take a solo. 'I was still trying to figure out the key they were in, never mind the tune. I played out of sheer terror. It must have been horrendous to listen to.' Spencer Davies didn't invite him to grace the stage much longer. Davies had a comeback to take care of, and he needed a fiddler in this condition like he needed a visit from his tax inspector.

Aly remembered the Davies débâcle some ten years later, when Stephane Grappelli, the jazz violinist, arrived in Edinburgh for a concert in the Usher Hall. Ed Baxter, the promoter, aware that the Boys of the Lough were playing in the same venue in a few days' time, phoned Aly on the afternoon of the Grappelli concert and said it would be good publicity for the Boys if Aly were to join the great man on stage at the end of the show and play a tune with him. Aly, who had revered Grappelli ever since, as a boy, he'd heard him on the classic Django Rheinhardt records of the Quintet of the Hot Club of Paris, went weak at the knees at the very thought of sharing the stage with him. He was a nervous wreck by the time he arrived at the Usher Hall, where Grappelli was already into his second-half set, playing like the wizard that he is. Aly's trepidation was understandable: there had been no rehearsal, he had no idea what Grappelli would want to play, and, what's more, he had never even set eyes on the man. As he sat in the dressing-room, listening to the superb music and the ovation that greeted every number, he felt like sneaking off home to hide. When he tried to tune up, he found he was shaking so much that he could hardly get the bow on to the fiddle strings. Luckily, Grappelli had for years been in the habit of drinking a couple of small malt whiskies before he went on stage – even a much-loved veteran virtuoso, it seems, has his moment of panic when it's time to face the music – and his barely touched bottle of Glenmorangie was standing beside his violin case. Aly seized the golden nectar and took a couple of big swigs. That, at least, took care of the shaking.

'When I walked on stage that night, I didn't know what to expect. I was totally at Stephane's mercy. I was terrified he was going to pick a hard key, because I knew that he loved to play in B-flat and all the other keys that are tricky on the fiddle. To this day, because I was so flustered at the time, I can't even remember what tune we played, although I think it was *Lady Be Good* [it was, in fact, *Sweet Georgia Brown*]. Whatever it was, he agreed to play it in G, which is a nice key for me. He took the first solo improvisation, and then it was my turn. He was supposed to come in after I had been through the tune twice, but he didn't. He made me take a third solo, and then a fourth, and then I realised he was never going to come in – he was just playing games with me. So I suddenly stopped at the end of a phrase, and he had to dive in to keep the thing going. I was running out of ideas. If I'd carried on, I would have made a fool of myself, and he obviously knew that. He was going to wait until I crucified myself. If

I'd had my wits about me, I would have started playing a reel or something after that. That would have taken the house down, and he would have been peeved. But I was so nervous, I couldn't think straight.'

Aly had, in fact, acquitted himself remarkably well in the circumstances, and as the audience cheered, Grappelli went over to him and flamboyantly kissed him on both cheeks. On the second kiss, the wily violinist paused long enough to whisper: 'Don't leave the stage yet. Remember, I'm the star!' Grappelli then took a succession of bows to rapturous applause and exited left, leaving Aly and the rest of the band to straggle off in the footsteps of the master.

These excursions were useful for Aly. They helped him to flap the fledgling wings of his solo career, and in a curious way they made him more appreciative of what the Boys of the Lough were doing. The Boys were in big demand throughout the 1970s, and continued with an unchanged personnel until 1979, when Robin Morton left the band. Aly and Robin had often been at loggerheads, not just over musical policy but also as strong-willed personalities with conflicting views. Aly was not unhappy to see Robin go, but the final parting was a sorrowful and acrimonious affair, with much talk about who had done what for the band, and what would have happened to them if this or that had not been done. Robin had done a great deal. He had given up a highly promising academic career, brought the Boys together, taken care of the business side of things and thrown his life into the band for almost a decade. Robin went off to build up his own record company, which he had begun on a small scale two years earlier in a converted church in Temple, Midlothian. He also took over management of the Battlefield Band, where he was able to use the skills that he had acquired while looking after the Boys' affairs. During the '80s, the Battlefield Band, fired by the brilliant multi-instrumentalist and songwriter Brian McNeill, were arguably the most popular folk group in Scotland, and they also toured the States, Europe and Australia to great acclaim – proof of Robin's management abilities. Robin was also director of the big, ten-day Edinburgh Folk Festival for several years.

The man who replaced Robin Morton in the Boys of the Lough was Tich Richardson, brother of Dave. The lanky Englishman was young and he was raw to the scene, but he could play guitar like an angel, and this certainly suited Aly, who had been reared on guitar or piano accompaniment and who, all these years, had been yearning for someone in the band to feed him some good old-fashioned Shetland chord sequences. 'He played roughly in the manner of Willie Johnson,' says Aly, referring to the Shetland guitarist who taught him so much. 'He had obviously listened to what Willie was doing, and it was great having him with us. He loved the music and, like us, he loved to travel to new places and meet new people, so he fitted in just fine.'

Tich's stay with the band was to be tragically cut short, however. Five years after joining the Boys, he was dead. He had always had a premonition of an early departure. Even at the tender age of thirty, he had made a will and even allocated a proportion of whatever there was in his estate towards the cost of a big party after his funeral. The Boys used to tease him unmercifully about his fears. He hated going in cars. He was sure they would crash. In September 1984, when the Boys were off duty, Tich went off to spend a few days on the Isle of Skye with Phil Cunningham who lived there at the time. One day, Phil had to take the car to Dingwall, on the mainland, and Tich joined him. They never reached their destination. Not far from Beauly Phil's car left the road and hit a tree. Tich's last words were: 'Oh, no!' His premonition had come agonisingly true.

Thankfully, Phil survived, although he suffered serious hand and arm injuries. After months of treatment by the doctors and some determined amateur psychological therapy by his splendid wife, Donna, he was eventually able to play again.

I remember the funeral in Newcastle. Phil, pale and bandaged, had made the courageous decision to be there. It must have been a terrible ordeal for him, and for Donna. There was a minister who knew Tich so well that he couldn't remember his real name. And Tich had his big party. We went through 120 bottles of Scotch, and for one night at least it was painless for just about everybody.

But the remaining Boys woke up the next morning to feel the despair of drowning men. At that point, there was a general consensus that they simply couldn't carry on. The Boys of the Lough were over. California, no more. Caledonia, no more. Good times, no more.

Cathal with Indian friends (Bombay, 1984)   *In the Land of the Rising Suntory (1984)*

'That nearly was the end of the band,' Aly recalls. 'We were all going through a deep depression. Cathal and I decided to leave it to Dave. If Dave wanted to keep the band going, then we'd go along with him.'

There were concert dates in the diary, and contracts had been signed. But in the end, what made Dave, Cathal and Aly resolve to soldier on was the positive feeling that it was what Tich would have wanted them to do. Not long after the funeral, the Boys were on the road again, playing their hearts out, playing for Tich.

Aly was numbed by Tich's death. 'He was a kind and sensitive man, too good to be taken away so early in his life. We all still miss him. Dave never really got over his death. In the end, it knitted us closer together and we became like the brothers we are. Tich's death made our commitment so much greater. It was so hard on Phil. We all gave him our support. He and Tich had been great friends.'

Aly pauses for a moment, his face clouded with remembered grief. 'Sometimes the world stinks,' he mumbles. 'The bad guys seem to live forever.'

In his time with the band, Tich had seen the world. It was a period of international expansion in the Boys' operations, with tours that took them to Australia and New Zealand, India, Japan and Hong Kong. On the American front, they pushed as far north as Alaska and as far south as Hawaii.

The Indian visit was really a stopover *en route* to Australia in 1984. The Boys had a concert date at the Tata Theatre in Bombay, and they were met at the airport by the organiser, Adi Sagar, who turned up in a Morris Oxford car, a model which had gone out of production in Britain many years previously. Aly told his host that the car wasn't in bad condition, considering how old it was. Mr Sagar was not amused. It was a brand-new vehicle, and what Aly didn't know was that India had continued to produce the Morris Oxford under licence long after the demise of the British version.

Like other visitors before him, Aly found India to be a country of baffling paradoxes and stark contrasts between rich and poor. But the Boys were treated like royalty, and for Aly, a curry *aficionado*, Bombay was culinary heaven.

The audience in the Tata Theatre was entirely Indian, with the solitary and highly visible exception of the French ambassador. The Boys were distinctly unsettled when they played their first set of tunes and saw a man get out of his seat and walk briskly towards the stage. They had visions of some dreadful revenge about to be taken for all the years of British colonial rule.

The man stood for a while gazing intently up at the band. Then, to their considerable relief, he politely applauded and returned to his seat. Someone else then did precisely the same, and then another and another . . . This ritual continued throughout the concert, and it turned out that it was the idiosyncratic Indian way of expressing admiration for a performance. The newspapers liked the music too, and there were stories about the concert – in the form of glowing reviews like the one which appeared in the *Indian Express*: 'Mr Bain's performance on the violin and Mr McConnell's wizardry on the flute and penny whistle was nothing short of virtuosity.'

After India, the Boys flew on to Japan, where their arrival was marked by yet another verbal *faux pas*. This time Dave was the culprit. It was snowing in Tokyo when the plane touched down, and Dave, as he shook the hand of the welcoming Japanese promoter, commented: 'This is a surprise. It's really nippy here!'

The Tokyo concerts had their amusing and bizarre moments, too. They were timed to start at around 5 p.m., so that people who had just finished work could come to the concert before going home. The theory was fine. In practice, what it meant was that many members of the audience, tired after a long day's toil, tended to fall asleep in the warmth and comfort of the theatre. The Boys soon discovered that the only way to rouse them was to get them singing. So Cathal would teach them the chorus of *The Rambling Irishman*. It wasn't a pretty sound, and the rest of the band had to leave the stage in fits of hilarity while Cathal bravely carried on through the high-pitched cacophony.

Another peculiarity of the Japanese music scene was that at the end of each concert, the band had to stand by the exit and bow and shake hands with the entire audience as they filed out, still happily humming oriental snatches of *The Rambling Irishman* and carrying their copy of the glossy programme, which contained meticulous transcriptions of the tunes in the Boys' repertoire, and details of the instruments — details which ranged from their general history right down to who had made the specific instruments that the Boys used. Back at the hotel, Dave and Tich, both of them six-foot tall, had some head-banging experiences as they struggled to get into their tiny rooms: they never did master the art of getting into a bath which was built vertically rather than horizontally in order to save space.

Aly has mixed feelings about the Japanese. They were wonderful hosts, treating the Boys to exotic dishes in the finest sushi restaurants, washed down with the local version of whisky. 'One night we had a drinking competition, although we didn't realise it at first. But it became obvious that they were trying to see if they could outdo us on the whisky.' When the Boys went to Japan they had all agreed not to mention the war — along the lines of the classic John Cleese episode in *Fawlty Towers*. But as more and more bottles of whisky went down that night, somebody did mention the unmentionable, and the Second World War was fought, verbally, all over again, with the Japanese arguing that their honourable soldiers were helping to free Asia from the corrupt colonial westerners. That night, the Boys did not win the war. But they did win the drinking competition, as one by one their hosts keeled over.

After the Far East sojourn, which included a concert at the Hong Kong Arts Festival, where their music was hailed by the *South China Morning Post* as having 'tremendous and meaningful vitality', the Boys flew to Australia for a string of concerts which ranged far across the vast country and took in New Zealand as well. It was an exciting, unforgettable tour. Somehow, word had got to the Aussies that the Boys of the Lough were worth a listen, and people flocked to the concerts, every one of which was a sell-out. Even in the Concert Hall in Perth, the Boys played to a capacity festival audience of some 2,000, and they were roared on by big crowds in Canberra, Adelaide, Melbourne, Sydney, Brisbane and Alice Springs.

Aly fell in love with Australia, its climate, its people, its food, its physical magnificence. The country was teeming with Scots and Irish expatriates, and they gave the Boys the kind of welcome that not even their fans in America could emulate. Aly recalls the Brisbane concert, where he asked the audience if there was anybody there from Shetland, and forty-two hands went up in the air. Wellington, New Zealand, did even better than that, with forty-seven. 'That's the most Shetlanders I've ever played to, outside Shetland itself, and there we all were, as far away from Shetland as you can possibly get. You wouldn't even find that many Shetlanders in Edinburgh.'

In the baking heat of Alice Springs, where you could swim in the hotel pool but not touch the sides of it without burning your hand, Aly heard of a ninety-five-year-old woman called Thompson who had been born there of Shetland parents and who wanted to meet him. Aly called on her, and the spritely old lady told him a remarkable tale. Her father was a fisherman in Shetland, and her mother had a premonition that he was going to be drowned at sea. The vision of future disaster was so overwhelming that she persuaded her husband to emigrate with her to Australia and settle in the place that was farthest from the sea. One day, he made the long journey to Sydney harbour to welcome some Shetland friends who were arriving by ship. While waiting at the harbour, he tripped, fell into the water and – you've guessed it – was drowned. 'The hairs rose on the back of my neck when she told me this,' says Aly. 'You can't escape your karma, as the Buddhists would say.'

Meanwhile, the only minor disasters that befell the Boys on that tour were caused by the extreme heat, which melted the glue on their instruments from time to time, literally leaving them with no strings attached. However, it was never as bad as the concert one year in Bermuda, when the Boys were playing outdoors and virtually all of the instruments fell to bits – the fiddle, the mandolin, the guitar. 'Even the concertina got clogged up,' says Aly, 'so Cathal sang songs until we had patched everything together again.' When Aly is travelling in hot countries he looks after his fiddle as if it were a baby. It is wrapped in damp cloths if the heat is dry. In humid conditions, the fiddle is always kept in an air-conditioned room.

By February 1985, there were more instruments to baby-sit than ever before. It was then, just a few months after Tich's death, that two Irish musicians, Christy O'Leary and John Coakley, were brought into the band to make it the five-piece that you can still hear today. Christy, born in County Dublin and brought up in Kenmare, County Kerry, not only plays Uillean pipes, tin whistle and harmonica but is also a fine singer. Christy was the first choice: it was he who recommended John Coakley, the first 'trained' musician that the Boys have ever had. John, from Cork, is a pianist, guitarist and fiddler who studied music at the University of Cork and also under the late Sean O'Riada. He was living in London when he got the Boys' call. John is not the most effusive of personalities, and when I asked Aly if John had jumped at the chance, he said: 'Well, put it this way, he joined of his own free will.'

John Coakley's piano accompaniment in particular gave Aly the kind of extra lift that he had long been wanting. 'The piano fills out the mid and lower ends of the music, and it's wonderful with slow airs and songs. And I liked the sound of Christy's pipes and his singing. Both Christy and John have become far better musicians through working with the band. They've both developed, and they're really into the music. And they're not restricted to Irish stuff. They're interested in all kinds of music. John and I have started to play a lot of Shetland tunes now on two fiddles. Both of them were made for the band. We are now five brothers instead of three. Their presence has encouraged our belief in what we do.'

There had always been Irishmen and a lot of Irish music in the Boys' repertoire. Inevitably, however, the presence of Christy and John considerably strengthened the Irish accent, a fact which has certainly done the band no harm in the United States, with its huge Irish-roots population. At home, though, there were some mutterings of discontent. I was one of the mutterers. I remember having a drink with Aly after a concert by the Boys in the Queen's Hall, Edinburgh, a few years ago and saying: 'Do you realise that here you are in the capital of Scotland, and you, the greatest Scots fiddler of your generation, only played one Scots tune all night?'

Aly, always a bonny fechter in the face of seemingly irrefutable argument, launched into a fiery defence of the musical policy, basically saying that it was all music, whether it came from Ireland or Scotland or Timbuktoo, and the Boys of the Lough played it better than anyone. Things were getting quite heated, until he concluded with a comment that had us both rolling around in laughter. If I attacked him in my *Scotsman* review, he concluded, 'du will be destroying the very monster that du created' – a reference to my early, encouraging writings about him at a time when the rest of the media weren't taking any notice. I was still smiling when I sat down to write the review, but Aly's protestation didn't alter a word: I stuck to my guns and made the same point that I had made in the bar that night.

Down Under (1984)

Beach Boys: Aly introduces Christy O'Leary and John Coackley to the rigours of touring in Hawaii

Cooking up a curry in New York with a hungry John Coackley patiently standing by

The new line-up in 1985, when Aly, Cathal and Dave were joined by Christy O'Leary and John Coackley

Since then, we have had many a long chat about the Irish connection, and occasionally, just occasionally, Aly has given a little ground and admitted that, in an ideal world, he would be playing more Scots music – 'but in a five-man group which is three parts Irish, what do you expect?' Besides, he finds plenty of scope for Scots music in his activities outside the band, and on a recent British tour with the guitarist Tom Gilfellon he didn't play a single Irish tune. Scots music, he argues, is not in any case entirely suitable to the band's instrumental line-up. 'It doesn't really work on flute and concertina, and for a long time we didn't have the accompaniment that Scots music really needs. Without a piano or a really strong guitar, it wasn't going to happen. Irish music suits the band better. It's easier to play without accompaniment. It's less formal. I actually like the formality of Scots music, which is an individual art form in its own right. It's got more sides to it than Irish music – the marches, the strathspeys and so on. But the Boys of the Lough are a band who just like music. They're not a Scottish band and never have been, even though most of us have lived in Scotland for many years.'

Ironically, the Boys of the Lough don't do a lot of work in Ireland itself, apart from the big annual festivals. That is partly to do with the economic situation there, and also because of the musical climate. 'The bands that are really popular in Ireland are more linked to American country music than anything else,' says Aly. 'There are a lot of great traditional bands – my own favourite is Altan – but, like us, they have to travel the world to make a living.'

At the same time, there are musicians everywhere in Ireland, including lots of tremendous traditional players who never reach the professional circuit and who seem quite content to confine their appearances to pub sessions. That's where Aly has most fun when he's in Ireland. He also admires the way the Dublin governments over the years have encouraged traditional culture. 'The Irish as a nation have taken their heritage and done a lot more with it than the Scots have. They've put money into it, and created a situation where traditional music is part of the everyday scene. You can hear it on the television adverts. You can hear it on an Irish airliner. It's much more a part of life than Scottish music in Scotland. The Scottish Tourist Board have never really wakened up to it.'

A clear indication that Irish music was to be a growing part of the life of the Boys of the Lough came in the title of album they recorded with Christy and John in the line-up for the first time. Issued in 1986, it was titled, in suitably green lettering, *Welcoming Paddy Home*.

The new Boys of the Lough went from strength to strength. As well as their instruments, which altered the whole texture and rhythmic balance of the sound in an attractive way, Christy and John brought with them material that served to freshen up the Boys' repertoire, Christy adding a further dimension to the concert programme with his fine singing.

And with the new sound came new outlets on the American circuit – towns and cities they had never been to before, bigger theatres and halls. By 1988, the Boys felt ready for their biggest, most important, gig of all.

The Boys of the Lough had been in existence in one form or another for twenty-one years. What better way to celebrate the event than with a show in New York's great Carnegie Hall? It began as a crazy notion over a few beers. But Ed Littlefield, owner of the new Sage Arts record label, believed it would make a great recording venue, and he and John Ullman, the Boys' American agent, soon set about turning the idea into reality. Within weeks, the deal was fixed for February — a concert by the Boys, with special guests Bill Monroe and the Bluegrass Boys, and a live digital recording of the momentous occasion.

Aly remembers that night as being the greatest thrill of his career. It was a thrill just to be there. The band went to the theatre on the afternoon of the concert for a sound-check. 'The hall has a special atmosphere and an aura of greatness about it. It made us all feel very humble to be standing on a stage that had seen so many legendary musicians. The acoustics were fantastic. As I played for the sound-check, I could almost watch the notes as they drifted towards the back of the hall.'

The Boys had fully expected to play to a half-full auditorium, but the crowds rolled in, and every seat was filled. Aly's heart was thumping as the writer and broadcaster Garrison Keillor, an old friend of the band, ran through a lengthy but hugely entertaining introduction, which included his own witty little song about the Boys of the Lough. Garrison got the audience beautifully relaxed, and, indeed, his intro was so good that it was used in its entirety at the start of the record, *Live at Carnegie Hall*.

If the Boys were nervous as mice in a catbox that night, there was nothing shaky about their music. They played as if their very existence depended on it — which, as Aly is quick to point out, it did! — and the fire and the passion seemed to spread to the audience, which roared its approval.

New York Times *advert for the momentous show at the Carnegie Hall*

Aly and Christy ready for take-off at Rennes, France, where the promoter got the local flying club to whisk the Boys off to their next concert

I once asked Aly to name just one of his own performances where the gods of music were with him, when something special happened to his playing, something that he might never be able to repeat again. He instantly went back to that night in Carnegie Hall, when he played *The Hanged Man's Reel*, a fiendishly tricky but very exciting tune he had learned from Jean Carignan. 'The acoustics were so good, and I was so wired up I felt as if I was about to explode. The music just came pouring out. After I finished the tune, it felt as if the house literally would be brought down, and the audience went on shouting and clapping for three or four minutes. The feeling afterwards was one of such relief and elation that, for once, I felt drunk without any alcohol.'

There was applause next day in the newspapers, too. The *New York Times* perhaps summed up the mood when it said: 'Aly Bain, the quintet's virtuosic fiddler, offered exuberant, shining solos in a programme whose arrangements also allowed the other players to exhibit highly developed individual skills.'

It was, of course, very much a team effort. Each man did his bit to make it work. But for Aly it was a personal landmark in his long musical odyssey. And the recording is there to prove it.

Chapter Five

SCREEN TEST

Aly Bain made his broadcasting début on radio when he was in his teens in Shetland. It wasn't a happy occasion. The BBC in those days had a programme on Scottish radio called *On Tour*, produced by Ben Lyons, and one day the tour took them to Shetland, where Aly and Ronald Cooper joined a crew of local and mainland performers in the village hall at Ollaberry in front of a hundred or so islanders, who had turned up because they knew the programme went out live on the air, and there was always the chance that something might go wrong.

It did. Just before it was Aly's turn to play a tune with some of his pals, a woman sitting next to him on stage collapsed with an epileptic fit and fell head-first into the audience. The boys had a half-bottle with them, but even that couldn't prevent them from playing what Aly describes as 'a jittery set'.

In the early '60s the television cameras arrived in Lerwick to film Tom Anderson's Forty Fiddlers, and looking at the picture of that session now, your eye is caught by Aly — he's the only youngster among them all. If a similar exercise were carried out today, the musicians would probably have an average age of about sixteen, such has been the explosion of fiddling among the youth of Shetland since Tom and Aly, in their separate ways, lit the fuse.

When he teamed up with Mike Whellans in 1969, Aly got occasional spots on television. One BBC producer, Ian McFadyen, was a great fiddle fan and he tried to work Aly into whatever was going. These three-minute flashes were a bit like commercial breaks, advertising fiddle music, and Aly accepted them willingly, whatever the format of the programme.

He was, in fact, hired for a real TV commercial in the early '70s. Douglas Eadie had been commissioned to put together an information advertisement for Ross and Cromarty County Council, in the north of Scotland, and had elicited the help of Owen Hand, appointing the Edinburgh folk singer as musical director. Owen roped Aly into the gig, and one day they went along to sort out the music. When they arrived at the studio they discovered that Douglas hadn't written anything. Possibly the subject-matter, which concerned the important role played by the vehicle passing places thoughtfully provided by the local authority on one-track Highland roads, had failed to get the creative juices going. Eventually, Douglas came up with the lines:

Along the roads of the north and west,
You'll find the scenery is the best.
So you don't want to drive so fast,
So never go stopping in that passing place,
Cos somebody needs that yard of space.

Sheer, unadulterated poetry, as somebody said at the time. Owen suggested delivering the dreadful words in the form of a talking blues, and a grateful Douglas Eadie invited the two musicians to appear on screen in the final version, which was to be filmed on the beautiful shores of Loch Maree in Wester Ross. Game for anything in those days, Owen and Aly agreed.

Owen recalls: 'We all got dressed up as straw-chewing hillbillies and piled into this 1928 Bentley and drove along the loch doing the song. I played banjo, with Aly busking along on fiddle, and the actor Billy Paterson did the words of the talking blues. I remember there was a problem in getting Aly into the picture. They had to get a box to bring him up to my height.'

After the filming, which happened to coincide with Aly's thirtieth birthday, the entire crew had a celebration knees-up ceilidh in the Loch Maree Hotel, where Owen got up for a dance and was birling a girl around at a furious pace when she unexpectedly let go. 'I finished up with my head going through a wall,' says Owen, 'but apart from that it was a great night.' Aly, too, had a sore head after the party, where the Highland malts had flowed in abundance.

The advert went on to become one of the best known on television in Scotland, because it eventually fell into the hands of the Scottish Office publicity people in Edinburgh, who had a television budget but nothing much to publicise with it, and who simply threw in the Loch Maree road show to fill the pre-booked prime-time viewing slots. It must have been the scenery that did it. The Ross and Cromarty Commercial – it always sounds to me like something you should be doing a rather elegant Scottish country dance to, without putting your head through a wall – may not have made a major impact on the safety-consciousness of the Scottish public, in spite of its countless showings on TV, but it did, at least, bring Douglas Eadie and Aly Bain together for the first time, and they became firm friends.

It was to be ten years, however, before Douglas and Aly were able to team up on another television project. This time the stakes were very much higher. For some time, Aly had been wrestling with the idea of somehow making a film based around some of the wonderful musical characters, notably the fiddle players, he had got to know in his north American travels. For their sixth album, *Good Friends, Good Music*, the Boys of the Lough had been joined by some of these American performers, including fiddlers Jay Ungar and Louis Beaudoin and the mandolin master, Kenny Hall, and it had worked well. Aly was convinced that a film treatment would work, too, but the television executives he approached both in Glasgow and London were scornful of the whole idea: it would cost a fortune . . . it wouldn't be worth the money . . . nobody had ever heard of these old guys anyway . . . it had only minority appeal . . . who wants to watch *folk* music these days? And so on.

It was Douglas Eadie who came to the rescue. He had been working with director Mike Alexander and cameraman Mark Littlewood, who had set up an independent programme-making company in Glasgow called Pelicula Films. Douglas set up a meeting between himself, Mike and Aly at Aly's house in Edinburgh. Mike, who already had some outstanding productions to his credit, recalls: 'Douglas told me later that Aly couldn't work out who I was. He thought I was maybe the television engineer.'

Mike and Douglas were excited by Aly's proposals 'And that,' says Aly, 'was that. On the same day, I made out a list of everybody I would like to film in the States. There were a lot of people on that list, but we eventually got them all except one.'

Channel 4, the new London-based commercial TV company, was still in its early days, with money to spend on a policy of alternative programming. Under the bold and imaginative leadership of Jeremy Isaacs, it was commissioning adventurous work from independent producers up and down the country. Mike, Douglas and Aly quickly put together a proposal and sent it off to Channel 4 in London, where at least one enlightened executive, Carol Haslam, loved the idea, even if Andy Park, a Scot who had been put in charge of light entertainment, was decidedly unenthusiastic.

'It's always struck me as weird,' says Aly, 'that the English like what you're trying to do in Scotland, while the Scots don't.' As it happened, Isaacs, too, was Scots-born, but he was not about to turn a good programme idea down, even one with as daunting a budget as this. 'It was absolutely unbelievable,' says Aly. 'Jeremy Isaacs and Carol Haslam pushed it through and suddenly we were in business.'

The musicians on Aly's list took a lot of tracking down. And the logistics of the filming arrangements were formidable – from Cape Breton to the Appalachian mountains and down to Texas – as the original plan behind the series was to explore the way country music had evolved in different parts of America and seek out any surviving connections with the Scots heritage.

Finally, in 1984, all was set for the first *Down Home* session. It took place near Nashville, at the ranch owned by the veteran Bill Monroe, generally regarded as the founding father of bluegrass music.

Aly was a bag of nerves. He had flown to the States on the previous day after a European tour with the Boys and had tried to conquer his jet-lag with a party at the hotel where the film crew were staying. 'That was a total mistake because we woke up next day feeling completely wiped out and when we reached Bill Monroe's ranch, I found we were going to do the filming in the open air, in a temperature of around 100 degrees.

'My knees were shaking. I had never interviewed anyone on television, or anything like that. The whole project had been partly my idea in the first place – who we should interview, who we should play with. And I thought, Christ, there's all these people out there – sixteen of us – what if I blow it and can't do it?'

Mike Alexander remembers what Aly went through that day. 'He was absolutely exhausted even before we started. It was a huge set-up – Bill Monroe and five other musicians – and Aly had to sit and talk with them and play tunes with them. Six hours in the broiling heat. I swear Aly shrank that day. He was getting redder and redder and visibly wilting. But he came through. It was an amazing display of resilience, because it was the first time he had done anything like this.'

To make things worse, Bill Monroe wasn't the easiest of interviewees, being in his late seventies then and very hard of hearing. Even if he did hear Aly, the touches of Shetland dialect baffled him. Monroe was seated at the opposite end of the line of musicians from Aly, who would shout across to him: 'Well, Bill, du plays the next tune.' To which Monroe would respond: 'Do what? Pardon?'

'That was an interesting but hard first day for me,' says Aly. 'But over the weeks as the process went on, I got used to it and in fact began to enjoy it. I loved working with Mike and Doug – they helped me so much.

'One of the many problems with Bill Monroe was that I had never met him before, and I found it difficult to interview somebody I didn't know. The rest of the series was fine, because I knew all the musicians well. Kenny Baker was on the Bill Monroe session. I had played with him a few times and admired his music a lot – he's an absolutely wonderful player on fiddle. Some people call him Stoneface, because he never smiles, so I decided to see if I could cheer him up. Bill didn't let his musicians drink on the job. If he saw them having a drink at any time in a professional situation, he fired them on the spot. But I had some duty-free malt whisky in the boot of the car, and sneaked round with Kenny and gave him a couple of big slugs. He cheered up immediately.'

Nashville was the scene of what came to be known as The Shoot-out. Mike and Douglas, who had arrived in town a few days before Aly, discovered that the brilliant young American fiddler Mark O'Connor was playing at a bar there. They went along to hear him. O'Connor wasn't on Aly's list, but Mike and Douglas were so astounded by his playing that they fixed up a filming date. 'Aly didn't know about it,' says Mike. 'When he arrived in Nashville, he was less than ecstatic to learn that he was expected to play with the hottest young fiddler in the States.'

Aly takes up the tale: 'Mark O'Connor is an absolute genius. I had first seen him in Washington when he was fifteen. He was an amazing player even then. He had learned his fiddle from Benny Thomson, who was a great Texas fiddle player, and he knew all the Texas swing, all those lovely fast Texas tunes and waltzes. The guys in the film crew were calling it The Shoot-out before we did the session. They were saying I'd meet my match with him. They were egging me on, trying to make me nervous. And succeeding! But it didn't turn out like that. What we actually did was *The Fairy Dance*, and he did his variations on it and I did my variations on it, and the only connection with a shoot-out was that it was incredibly fast.'

Mike Alexander reckons that O'Connor was impressed, too, although fiddle players the world o'er seem to find compliments easier to receive than to give. 'During rehearsal I saw them in the corner of the bar, and Aly was showing O'Connor some things on the fiddle, like the dancing bow technique which he hadn't seen before. They made an odd couple – Mark is as long as Aly is short. And I remember Aly doing his dancing-bow thing and then looking up at Mark, who said just one word: "Wow!" Mark is a very laconic guy, and that, for him, was the height of praise.

'Being able to play was the secret of making these films,' says Aly, 'because I could go in with these guys, and as soon as they knew I could play they completely relaxed and realised that everything was going to be okay because I understood the music and had a feeling for it. We weren't going to produce some bullshit. It was going to be good, and they knew what we were looking for. If I'd just been a television presenter and not a musician, it wouldn't have worked at all.'

Mike agrees. '*Down Home* was in a way ahead of its time because it didn't use the accepted documentary form, it used performance. What makes Aly's films different is that he's a musician and he's talking to friends and playing with friends, and it creates a different kind of atmosphere. Obviously, to begin with he was nervous, but I think if we looked at one of the *Down Home*s and then looked at the last thing we did in Shetland, we'd see he had progressed enormously.

'What you do get from Aly is what nobody else I've seen on music documentaries can do – they can do one thing or the other, but they don't have the musicianship or they don't have the standing that Aly has. I mean, to go right round America and meet the players that he's played with at all these festivals and sit down and talk and play with them in front of a camera – whether it's swing or Appalachian or whether it's Canadian – you name it, he can do it. So that makes it the epitome of music having no

Another Down Home *session, with Johnny Gimble and Junior Daugherty*

boundaries. It's an old cliché, but he actually is the epitome of it, and he brings it to the screen. That unique talent – the way he plays the music, the way he brings musicians out of themselves – is something he's done which nobody else has done.'

What the American musicians didn't know was that Aly had been listening to their music and playing it since he was a boy. 'When I met Johnny Gimble and played the Bob Wills stuff, he couldn't believe that I wasn't American. But I'd learned the tunes of all the Bob Wills records years ago. I loved the music, and because of that I think I got a feel for it. So I fitted right into the American scene.'

Johnny Gimble, who had started his career with Bob Wills and the Texas Playboys, was at that time the Mr Nashville of fiddle music – a title that has since passed to Mark O'Connor. Aly visited him at his home in Austin, Texas, before the filming session, along with Junior Daugherty. 'We ended up playing swing music and Bob Wills music, and I played some Scots fiddle, which I don't think Johnny Gimble had heard much of before. He set up a tape recorder and taped lots of the stuff I was doing, so I suppose he must have liked it.'

Later, Aly and the crew went to Montreal to film the great French-Canadian, Jean Carignon. 'Carignon was old and not in the best of health, and his ear had gone a bit, but he could still handle the fiddle. When we were in his house the day before the filming he seemed very sort of downcast and unforthcoming. I don't think his wife really liked the music. But next day, as soon as we got into the car he sort of came to life and he produced a bottle of whisky – he wasn't really allowed to drink in the house. We had a couple of drinks from his bottle, and I had one, too, so he was delighted, and that made the whole shoot a success.

'He loved every minute of it. I remember him saying to me that he was allowed to drink some whisky because his blood was too thick, and the whisky would help to thin it. "I'm going to have a stroke some day," he told me, and that's exactly how he died not long after we filmed him.'

Carignon, though far past his peak, was still acknowledged as the master of the fiddle. Aly certainly acknowledged it: 'He was undoubtedly the best fiddler that lived this century at what he did, which was a mixture of French-Canadian, Irish and Scottish music which he had learned off 78s when he was a kid. The Irish stuff he'd learned from Michael Coleman. The Scottish stuff had come from Scott Skinner. He was such a brilliant fiddler that he had taught himself all the techniques – he was just incredibly gifted naturally. And I thought, Jesus, I'm going to have to sit and play with this guy. I had played with him before, but I had always been in awe of him. He was a genius.

'There were several tunes I wanted him to play, like the great French-Canadian tune called *The Awakening of the Birds*, which is a kind of virtuoso fiddle piece which is very beautiful and very difficult to handle. And I wanted him to play *The President*, the Scott Skinner tune which is really classical in form. He did it all easily. It was no problem to him. When I played, I knew there was something I could do which he couldn't do, and that was play reels with long notes in them, because all his music was very fast, with the notes really clipped.

'Carignon noticed what I was doing, and he said: "How do you get them long notes?" So I showed him, and he got it right away, as you would expect. And then he looked at me and said: "You've improved. Your bowing's improved since the last time I saw you. Yes, you're getting better." From him, that was the ultimate compliment. He didn't hand them out easily.'

Among the assorted characters featured in *Down Home* was a wonderful black singer called Elizabeth Cotton, who was then into her nineties but as lively as a kitten, playing upside-down guitar and singing her famous composition, *Freight Train*, which had sparked off the astonishing British skiffle boom in the '50s. Lots of other transatlantic connections were discovered as the crew moved round north America — Jean Ritchie singing a song to the same tune as *MacLeod's Reel*, Bill Monroe playing *Scotland*, the elderly J.P. Frayley reminding Aly that the fiddle used to be known as 'the devil's box' in the Kentucky Bible-belt while in Scotland it was 'the devil's instrument'. But any idea of pursuing the original game-plan of concentrating on musical links between the New World and the Old was soon abandoned. 'We quickly found as we filmed that we had to keep it loose,' says Aly. 'The music was so varied, you just had to let it happen.'

In Cape Breton, of course, with its large population of Highland descendants, Aly found the transplanted flower of Scotland still blooming. 'We filmed three old guys waulking the tweed and singing Gaelic songs just as their ancestors would have done on the island of Barra in the nineteenth century.'

When it came to interviews, however, the Cape Bretons were not exactly riveting. A typical exchange would go like this:

Aly:	Have you ever been to Scotland?
Cape Breton:	Yeah.
Aly:	What do you think of the Scots fiddling over there?
CP:	It's fine.
Aly:	Well, we really like your music. How did you learn it in the first place?
CP:	From the guy next door.
Aly:	Did he teach you some Scottish tunes?
CP:	Yeah.

'The interview side of it was a nightmare, and I would come out in a cold sweat. I'd spent all these weeks talking to people like Jean Carignon, who could talk till the cows came home, and it was hard to get them to shut up. The Cape Bretons were entirely different — nervous, reclusive types who didn't like to boast or brag. But once they started to play, they burst into life.'

They filmed a dance at Glencoe, where the hall sits on a hill on its own, miles from nowhere. 'When I got there, I thought who on earth is going to turn up in this place? But suddenly hundreds of cars started arriving out of the blue and surrounded this

Aly meets the Cajuns: D.L. Meynard (left) and friends during filming at D.L.'s house

little hall like Indians circling round a wagon train. On stage, there was just Buddy McMaster playing the fiddle with the traditional piano accompaniment. But the crowd started this amazing step-dancing, and Buddy played on and on, for something like five or six hours. There was a sort of space between the dance floor and the earth. Louis Kramer, the sound man, wanted to get a good recording of the rhythm of the dancing, so he and I crawled underneath and I remember watching the dance floor heaving up and down to the music about a foot at a time.'

After the North American material was in the can, the crew moved to Shetland, where Aly was able to resume his old musical partnership with Tom Anderson, Willie Johnston and Violet Tulloch. He was back among his ain folk, and he felt a tremendous sense of relief. It had been a long, hard slog. 'It was hard on my nerves, but it was a great experience and I'm really glad we did it, because what we achieved with *Down Home* was a little bit of history. Only the crew, Mike, Doug and I will ever know what went into the making of it.'

Down Home went out on Channel 4 in March 1986 as a weekly series of four hour-long programmes at prime time. The critics were impressed, and so were Channel 4 when they saw the viewing figures.

Unfortunately, for contractual reasons, the show never got an airing on American television. As Aly points out: 'We made the fundamental mistake of not buying out the performers' rights completely. In order to show the films in the States a television company would have to renegotiate the contracts of all the musicians. One of these days, though, Americans will get to see it, because of its historical importance. Some of the musicians are dead now, and they've taken their music with them. You could show *Down Home* again in sixty years time, and it will still be as valid as when we shot it, probably even more so.'

Even while Mike, Douglas and Aly were working on *Down Home* they were formulating their next project for television. It began with Douglas's idea of a film called *From Ice to Water*, which would tell the story of the French-speaking Cajuns from the time they were sent packing by the British out of Nova Scotia and Canada to the time they were pushed out of the New Orleans area into the hot swamplands of Louisiana. Back in London, though, things had changed at Channel 4, and they weren't signing cheques for £350,000 with quite the alacrity of before. But all was not lost. Channel 4 were looking for an offbeat programme to put out on New Year's Eve, something that would make people switch over from the wearisome bonhomie of the paper-hatted kitsch which television invariably purveyed on Hogmanay. They invited tenders from the independent filming companies. At the Edinburgh Television Festival, they announced the winning entry. It was from Pelicula, and it was to be a film of Aly Bain and the Cajun musicians of Louisiana. The rival bidders gathered in the Assembly Rooms could hardly believe their ears.

For Aly and his colleagues, it was a compromise. It was not the musical

With producer Doug Eadie, American manager John Ullman and Mark Littlewood

123

documentary that they had envisaged, involving lots of location shooting and interviews with the reigning kings of Cajun. It had to be up-tempo, it had to be music all the way, and it had to be squeezed into one sixty-minute slot. At the same time, they were full of admiration for Channel 4's bravery in supporting their cause even to this limited extent. The filming was done in 1988, and once again Aly found himself playing side by side with some of his musical idols, notably the veteran fiddler Dewey Balfa, whose band, the Balfa Frères, had waved the flag for Cajun music back in the mid-'40s, and who was one of the first Cajun performers to be featured at the Newport Folk Festival.

Playing with Dewey gave Aly one of the biggest musical kicks of his career. 'To end the film, I wanted something sad but lovely. I had met Dewey Balfa and D.L. Meynard at the Mariposa Festival in Toronto in the early '70s. We got on great together. Dewey was such a sincere, emotional man. I loved their music. They, like us, were trying to establish their culture on a wider basis. When we came together all these years later, I remembered one lovely song that they had done at Mariposa called *As I Passed Your Door*. We looked around the little town of Eunice, where we were filming, and found an old bar where all the rednecks were gambling. They didn't like the interruption, but it was nice and seedy, and just the right place for us. D.L. sang and played guitar, Dewey played melody and I played harmony. The music and the atmosphere were perfect. For me, it was a magical moment – something I can still feel as I sit at home and watch the tape.'

Even the tight-lipped D.L. Meynard, the 'Cajun Hank Williams' of Louisiana Aces fame, seemed unusually affected by the session. Generally, if D.L. spoke to you at all it was a great mark of respect. But he turned to Aly and drawled: 'Aly Bain, you dirty dawg!' Aly, who wasn't quite certain how to take the remark, was quickly assured by the other musicians that this was just about as gushingly effusive as D.L. had sounded about anything or anybody in years.

After *Aly Meets the Cajuns*, Aly found plenty more television work waiting for him at home in Scotland, and somehow he managed to cram it in while still keeping his touring commitments with the Boys of the Lough. *Aly Bain and Friends*, made by Scottish Television in Glasgow in 1989, featured him in his now accustomed dual role of link-man and musician. Among the guest performers was his old friend from the London recording studios, Richard Thompson. A further series followed, after which Aly turned his thoughts to Shetland, where he had long wanted to do a major television production. The annual Shetland Folk Festival, which attracted musicians from the States and the British Isles as well as a galaxy of local talent, was the obvious springboard, and the three musical musketeers who had so succesfully invaded America – Aly, Mike Alexander and Douglas Eadie – got together again and started touting around for sponsorship.

I remember meeting Aly some time in the early part of 1991. He was just off the plane from a trip to Shetland and he was clearly in the mood for a celebration. 'What's the big occasion?' I asked.

'The big occasion, my friend, is that after a whole year of negotiating we've managed to get funding for the Shetland sessions.' The cost was to be shared between Shetland Folk Festival, BBC Scotland and BBC 2.

In May of that year, Aly and the team flew to Shetland to embark on a frenetic schedule, which all had to be wrapped up in the space of ten days. 'In just over a week,' says Aly, 'we shot twenty miles of film and recorded seventy-three numbers.'

Again, Aly was operating under extreme pressure, but came across on screen as naturally as ever. Mike Alexander is still amazed at how quickly Aly got to terms with what is required for television in a highly professional way and yet never lost himself in the process. Mike recalls: 'We shot six half-hour programmes in ten days, involving twenty-five or thirty different filming sessions, and I don't think anybody can grasp just how much work Aly has to put in to make that possible. He picks the musicians, he works out the tunes, who will play what and when, who should sit where, and so on. Nothing like that can be as casual or relaxed as it looks. The work has to go in to make sure the chemistry is right – which is what Aly does. To get to that stage of understanding and trust is what makes it such a joy to make these programmes and films with him. It makes it different from anything else.'

The Shetland Sessions had music from each of the main festival performers, who included D.L. Meynard, Graham Townsend, Danny Thompson, Phil Cunningham, Eddie Le Jeune and Gerry O'Connor, together with local stars like Hom Bru, the

Strength in numbers: Pelicula's full Shetland Sessions *production team*

'I told you we should have had a rehearsal.' The Shetland Sessions, *with Phil, Willie Hunter, Violet and May Gair*

Shetland Fiddlers, Young Heritage, and another of Aly's old fiddle mentors, Willie Hunter. The BBC found that the combination of sparkling music and superb scenic shots of Shetland proved so popular that they screened all six programmes a second time in 1993.

At the time of writing, there are other television plans being laid, but Aly finds that it is getting continually harder to raise the kind of funds that his television ideas demand. 'It's not just a simple business of putting a few musicians into a studio and getting each of them up for two or three minutes to play the fiddle or the accordion. I'm not interested in that sort of programme. If the TV people in Glasgow want to carry on doing that, then they're welcome to do it. What I want to do is to take television out of Glasgow and into the areas where the music is played. You've got to get a sense of the geography, why people are playing, and how the music fits into the community – that's very important, and it's what really interests me. But it's always going to be a very expensive way to make television programmes, because you have to be travelling and filming on location all the time. Hopefully, things will change and the people who matter will realise that there's no substitute for quality.'

Chapter Six

ALY BAIN AND FRIENDS

BILLY CONNOLLY

The Scottish folk scene in the 1960s provided a young former shipyard worker in Glasgow with his first professional platform. Billy Connolly's ambition then was to be a banjo player who sang mainly American country-style songs, with a few jokes thrown in along the way. He formed a highly successful group called the Humblebums. But it wasn't long before his outrageous sense of comedy came bursting out in a spectacular shower of jokes and patter, and he went on to become Scotland's outstanding comic, with a vast, devoted following that stretched across the world. He has appeared in films and television sit-coms on both sides of the Atlantic. Billy has had good cause to be wary of the press, especially on home territory; luckily, he knew me from the Humblebum days and during a break from filming in Glasgow in April 1993 he invited me to his hotel to talk at length about his old friend, Aly Bain.

I used to go to the folk club in Glasgow. It was in the Grand Hotel, a lovely big Victorian building that doesn't exist anymore. One night I went along and Aly was the guest. He had never seen people like me before. I was a headcase in those days. I was wearing capes, long hair and weird clothes. And there was Aly, straight from Shetland, in a wee V-necked pullover and a wee shirt. And he just blew everyone away. I had never heard a fiddle played like that before. I had never heard the clarity of tone or the volume from a fiddle before. I had never heard that *passion* on a fiddle.

It always seemed a dull instrument to me, played by dull guys who had learned it at dull schools. But Aly was different. He played an American tune I loved called *Maple Sugar*. I just couldn't believe it, and I spoke to him afterwards. He was actually quite scared of me. He must have wondered: what's the problem with this guy? That was the first time I met him. He went back to Shetland after that, and then later he came down to Glasgow to live. I found him scraping around trying to get gigs, and the ones he got were rotten gigs. Nobody wanted to book a solo fiddler. It was all singers and groups. It was a very pullovery time, you know. People were all wearing the same clothes,

A Who's Who of all the big names on the folk scene in 1969 at the Inverness Folk Festival, where Aly and Mike had their first major success. Back (left to right): Billy Connolly, Gerry Rafferty, Hamish Henderson, Hamish Bain, Jean Redpath, Archie Fisher, Finbar Furey, Aly, Tam Harvey, Derek Moffat. Front: Cyril Tawney, Eddie Furey, Tich Frier, Andy Ramage, Ian McCalman. Happily, they're all still alive and kicking

bands were wearing the same outfits – red shirts and grey flannels. We were never into it.

Towards the end of the '60s I had been in a band called the Skillet Lickers, doing strictly old-timey American, and it was brilliant. I did things on my own, playing autoharp and banjo and singing Carter Family songs and Jimmy Rodgers stuff, and it was going down rather well. Then I met Tam Harvey, who was a plectrum guitarist who had played in rock bands, and he liked country music. I didn't like being solo, so we got together and formed the Humblebums. And then Aly appeared from Shetland and I said: 'Why don't you join us, and it'll get you exposure. We'll just split the bread three ways instead of two.' This didn't please Tam a great deal. Tam was a kind of money man. You know, guys are all different. I thought I was a hippy. I was in for the big game. I thought the world was going to change – and it did. I thought we were all part of something very exciting and alternative.

But Tam always looked on it in a more constructive way – that he might be able to buy a house, or get married, or buy a car and all that. That never crossed my mind. I always had a sort of conceited, arrogant idea that I was going to be famous anyway, so everything would look after itself in the end. It's a thing I still hang on to. It's that if you excel, you get the prizes anyway. They may stop you for a wee while. But at the end of the day they're going to need you. It never dawned on me that it might end. I felt indestructible – I was going to live forever. Forward, ever forward! The scene was too healthy to fold up tomorrow. It might do so in two years, but God knows where we would be then.

Anyway, I knew Aly had to be in the band. I knew in my soul that we had to help this guy. You mustn't let this man wander about getting half-arsed gigs as a solo fiddle player and then catch the plane back to Shetland. This mustn't be allowed. This would be wrong. So I got him in.

Those first gigs with Aly were brilliant. He was incredibly unique. He would burst into American country or Cajun-sounding stuff, or stuff he'd learned from records, but he played it with exactly the same passion as he would play his own Shetland music. We were doing weird things like *Windy and Warm*, Chet Atkins things, and things like *Cripple Creek*. And Aly loved it. And then he would do *Sweet Georgia Brown* with the same passion. So he never saw the change of material as a step up or a step down – it was merely a sidestep and into it, lads, one, two, three, four . . .

I couldn't play *Sweet Georgia Brown*. I didn't know the chords. So I would step aside and Aly and Tam would do it. Tam could do all those Django Reinhardt chords, and it really gave Aly a chance to shine in Stephane Grappelli style. So the band would change in character, and the mood would change. And it suited me fine, because I'm really a storyteller. So I would tell a story, and off we'd go again, back to being the Humblebums, with me crashing about on the banjo.

He was a delight to be with. He was a shy country boy who'd fallen among thieves. I'm not a hard man by any manner of means, and neither was Tam Harvey. But we were both city boys, and we could do our share – you know, I wasn't scared. I didn't *want* to fight anyone. But we were always having to punch people in Indian restaurants – sort people out. Aly had just come down from Lerwick and he was terrified all the time he was with us. He'd never seen people fighting. He'd never seen people being smacked on the mouth. He'd never seen *casual violence*. I would say: 'Excuse me a minute, Aly,' and *bang*, I'd belt somebody. He'd say: 'My God! What's happening?' And I would explain to Aly that if I didn't hit the guy now, I would hit him three hours later, but by then we'd both be seriously pissed off. So if you hit him now, it goes away. I was trying to teach him the city ways. Aly always used to say I walked in a weird way. I used to walk as if I was challenging the world. I'd wear an Arab striped coat and pink and white striped trousers, with my hair shaggy and sticking out, and people would look at me and I'd say: 'What are you looking at, you bastard?' Aly couldn't believe this aggressive approach. We took it on stage. Aye, right! And Aly loved that bit.

I remember one gig at the Glasgow Folk Centre. I said to Tam and Aly: 'Okay, guys, you play *Sweet Georgia Brown* while I go and get the money.' There was only a sheet of hardboard separating the stage from the back office. In the middle of *Sweet Georgia Brown* – *bang*! The negotiations had begun. The difference between the actual fee and the actual folding fun tickets hadn't added up, so you had to go through the pockets of this guy – I won't name him. It was always in the same pocket – up in that top pocket where you put your pens. Eric Cuthbertson, the blues player, tells me that the first time he met me he was coming up the stairs of the same folk club, and I was holding the organiser outside the window. Meaningful discussions were taking place on the window ledge. I was inside the building, and the guy was looking at Glasgow from an upside-down position. Tam Harvey was in the street, catching any change that fell out of his pocket. It was a very funny period.

I had a motorbike and sidecar. A BSA Shooting Star. And we used to load it up and go off to the gig, with Tam usually in the sidecar. I preferred Aly sitting behind me, because Tam had no idea of balance – he had never danced, or anything like that. He knew how to balance a cheque-book account, and he knew all about music – he knew every note on the keyboard – but he nearly killed us on many occasions. Roundabouts were a nightmare. Tam would keep trying to sit up straight.

We would go and play not just in folk clubs but in miners' welfare clubs and social clubs. Aly thought these places were like stepping into Hades. But he just shone, and the people loved him. He was a very attractive man when he was young – big eyelashes and big, doe eyes. Women used to just melt. He had never had much experience in the social graces, but he suddenly found that he was naturally endowed with them, and women just loved him, because his soul was in his music, and they bought it lock, stock and barrel. You could hear the cash register going *ding*!

I got jealous of him one night. We were playing at Prestwick and a woman came in. She was a relative of a fellow called Ian Campbell, who was driving us around. Little Ian was the nephew of Matt McGinn, the Glasgow songwriter, and a relative of his had a second-hand shop or something and had a pair of cowboy boots for sale. Aly had always thought I was kind of weird because I always wore cowboy boots. He had never seen them before. All I was really doing was copying Alex Campbell. The cowboy boots became my trademark, because Alex wasn't around too much and it looked kind of original. Anyway, this relative of Ian's turned up with a pair of cowboy ankle boots the likes of which I'd never seen. They were beautiful, pointy things with big heels. Try as I might I couldn't get them on. It was like the Ugly Sisters all over again. My veins were sticking out on my forehead trying to get my stupid big foot into this wee boot. God, they were lovely boots. And Aly said: 'Oh, there's a nice pair of boots,' and slipped them on like they'd been made to measure. I could have killed him.

But he wore them, and I'll tell you he changed when he wore those boots. You remember when you first put on a dinner suit, with a bow-tie and all that, and you start walking like Cary Grant? That happened to Aly. It was the day he became tall. He was a different character. You know, until then he was a bit Marks and Spencer. He's remained that way. He's a bit utility, is our Aly. He's got a stay-pressed look about him.

What's never changed has been the way he has always looked good when he plays. Aly has that wonderful thing that great musicians have – his body goes the way his music takes him. It's not a preconceived affair, it just happens. I think people who concentrate totally on what they do — on the excellence of what they're doing — they always look good.

I loved him because he was such a barrel of complexities. He was a simple country boy — I mean that in the fondest sense, because he's not simple at all. But he was also a political leftie — all the way from Shetland. We used to howl with laughter when he told us how the Communist Party would meet back home in the police station or somewhere on Friday nights. So he had the same political passion as us. The difference was that he was driven solely by his *conscience*. We were driven by conscience, too, but we were shipyard guys, industry people. We had the Red Clyde to think about, and we behaved as our peers did. But he was behaving as his conscience took him, which was a much purer thing than ours. We've all grown up a bit since, and the world has changed a bit, but we've both remained pretty much with the same ideals.

I met him in Melbourne a few years ago. He was playing there and he saw my show advertised and he got in touch. He looked so awkward. He just had those clothes that he wears — those Shetlandy things. He was sweating away. I had a pair of psychedelic shorts — red, yellow and green — and I lent them to him. He was deeply embarrassed, but to his eternal credit he went along with it, and we went and sat on the beach. And he says: 'I cannae believe you. We're in the tropics. We're sitting here in these ridiculous clothes, and you're talking about a bad write-up you got in the paper in Cumbernauld.' And I was! 'You're a complicated man,' he says, shaking his head.

There was this thing about him coming from Shetland that made him so different. I was talking to Peerie Willie [Johnson] years ago, and it turned out that Willie had been brought up on an island and he made his first visit to the mainland when he was twelve. He had never seen a baby! Aly had never seen a train! That's what we're talking about. That passion thing is derived from all sorts of angles, but when you understand the way they lived, and the isolation, you realise why their music is so good, why they're so intense about it, because they didn't have any telly, they only had their little radios and harmoniums and guitars and fiddles. I met an old lady in Shetland who had never been to Lerwick — she said she felt she couldn't take the pace! I found it really charming. I'm not saying that as a putdown, because she was a much more complete person than I am. But it blew me sideways, and it does tell you a great deal about the intensity and the passion thing. They're much more in touch with their souls — if we do have such a thing — than we are with ours, or certainly were until our generation. They don't have the distractions that we have, so they're much more pure. Now they have the tellies and the satellites and they get CNN, and I don't know what it will do to them, because Oprah Winfrey isn't going to improve the way of life in Shetland.

It took me years and years to get to Shetland, and when I got there to do a show Aly happened to be there. He was making an album with *Margaret's Waltz* on it. They played me the track and I said: 'Play it again, play it again,' until they were all going crazy. It's stunning. That Shetland trip was one of the nice times in my life. Aly turned up, to my deep joy, at the concert with Violet Tulloch. I didn't know all those great guys were in the audience — Willie Hunter and everybody. And Aly said: 'The lads say they loved your concert, and they've got a wee do for you afterwards.' So we went along to Violet's house and we all sat around drinking at first. I didn't take my banjo – I was too scared. There was a lot of whisky drinking and a lot of laughing going on. Eventually, when they'd all had a skinful they got out their instruments and played – my God, how they played. They played till three or four in the morning. It was such a gas, Aly and Willie and all of them, soaring into heaven. It was the most astonishing thing I've ever witnessed. They're like rock and roll people – they get pissed first, and then they play.

All the musicians and singers I've loved – people like Gerry Rafferty, Tam Harvey, Rab Noakes, Calum Kennedy – they all have something where at night I'll say: do that thing, sing that thing or play that thing. With Aly I would always say: play *Niel Gow's Lament for His Second Wife*, and it still makes me cry inside. The tears don't roll down my cheeks. But when he plays, something inside me lies down and goes to sleep. He's magnificent. His passion is something I've never experienced in another fiddler – Yehudi Menuhin doesn't do it to me, no other fiddler does it to me. Ravi Shankar can do it, and Eric Clapton and Chuck Berry. All of these guys, they all have a sound that belongs to them. And they can get it from *your* instrument, but you can't get it from theirs. They own the sound. Bert Jansch owns his sound, you know. And Aly owns his, and he can get it out of any old cheap fiddle.

He always does something that just takes my bloody breath away, even at this late stage in the game. I went to the Traverse Theatre last year to see him with Norman MacCaig, and I went in fear and trepidation – there's this rather shy man who plays fiddle like an angel, and there's this guy who writes a great deal better than he speaks. And I thought, my God, what's going to happen here? But one's love for the other just exploded on stage. It was great. I was so glad. I felt so privileged to be there. Later, Aly said it would be nice for him and me to do a show like that, and I'd love to do it some day. I want to play *Margaret's Waltz* with him on autoharp, because the first time I heard the tune I went straight away and learned it.

He and I played together in the Humblebums for about a year or a year and a half. Then he began straining at the leash, as was very natural and proper. He started playing little bits and pieces with other guys, and then along came Mike Whellans, and it was a marriage made in heaven, I thought. When Aly moved to Edinburgh I didn't see much of him, although we used to get together at festivals and things and have a lot of fun.

Edinburgh always had strange guys coming out of the woodwork and then disappearing back into it – a lot of guitarists, people like Owen Hand. But they didn't want to be performers. People in the west of Scotland always wanted to be performers. Everybody wanted to be a star, to be Josh Macrae or Alex Campbell, to be funny – like Hamish Imlach – but the Edinburgh guys wanted to be in the library. I didn't want any books written about me – I wanted to be on the front page of the newspaper (Jesus Christ, I got that!). But, then, so did Jimmy Boyle. I used to go to the traditional folk clubs dressed the way I did and nobody batted an eyelid. They'd say, oh here's that banjo player, the half-wit. They never asked me to sing. They used to go right along the row of singers and skip me. They were all callin' the yowes tae the knowes. It was all that Ewan MacColl crap, and it bored me stiff. I never wanted to be Earl Scruggs: I wanted to be a guy who played banjo rather well, but who was also funny. I desperately wanted to be funny. And it was only when Aly came into the band that he gave the music credibility and set up a platform for me to do what I wanted to do.

He was the first great instrumentalist and the best ever. There's just one Aly in every generation. For me, Aly is Miles Davis. He's Ravi Shankar. He's Bella Fleck. He is in that number, and he's completely unaware of it. That's what gives him this lovely strength, and that's what will sustain him forever. In the '60s, as Joe the punter who was listening to the Grateful Dead as well as Hank Williams and all that stuff, I chanced on this bloody fiddler and thought: what is this? I don't know what I heard — just this sweetness, this beauty, this undeniable beauty. What you get from Aly is excellence, and you think, my God, I'm in the presence of something awfully good. When he first came to Glasgow he was really just a boy, although he was about twenty-one. But even then he knew every tune you could think of. People would say: 'Oh, do you know the *Reel for Mrs McConachie on the Occasion of Her Second Son's Marriage to Margaret Lawson*? And he'd say: 'Oh aye,' and off he'd go.

Aly was alone. There was no beast such as Aly. There was no guitarist as good as he was on fiddle. There was no banjo. The song was the thing then, and everybody who played was a kind of accompanist. After Aly, the only other guy I can think of who took my breath away and who could do something I'd never seen in my life before is a guy called [Phil] Cunningham and he plays the accordion. Cunningham blew my mind when I first saw him. You chance across greatness, you get a flash of it, a second of it, and you don't know where it came from or how the hell they got it. But they've got it. They know the hotspot on the instrument.

Nobody shone like Aly, or the Cunningham guy later. And Aly's still shining. Ask the people out there in the streets how many fiddlers they know. His name's first on the lips every time. That's an amazing achievement. Like all the great players have done, he's made people like not just the music he plays but the instrument itself.

We've come and gone, and we've fallen out a few times, but he's still my dear, dear friend, and I love him.

PHIL CUNNINGHAM

As a schoolboy, Phil was the fastest accordionist in the east of Scotland, possibly in the universe, and even his first band, Silly Wizard, no slouches in reel time, could hardly keep up with him. He has matured into a superb all-round musician with several solo albums in which he plays piano and whistle as well as the notorious 'box'. He has taken to composition, too: he provided the music for Bill Bryden's spectacular 1990 presentation of The Ship *in Glasgow, and has written many memorable tunes that have found their way into the folk repertoire. He is also much in demand as a producer in the recording studio, which is where I found him for this interview. His appearances as a performer have become few and far between, although he still teams up with Aly Bain for an annual Scottish tour.*

With Phil at Eden Court Theatre, Inverness (1992)

The first time we ever got together to plan a tour we were up in Skye, where I lived, and we decided we'd need something like twenty different sets of tunes to do on this tour. We spent two days working on it, and at the end of the two days, we only had three bloody sets. I thought to myself, this is ridiculous – with all the tunes that he knows and all the tunes that I know, we're bound to be able to think of more than three sets. But we couldn't. So we went into the bar at Floodigarry and got legless and had a session, and the tunes started coming out. As each one was played, I was quietly writing down the titles on a piece of paper without letting Aly know what I was doing.

Next day, I pulled out the list from the night before and we suddenly had about sixty tunes that we could put in the programme. Once you get Aly into a session, the tunes just come piling out.

We were talking about it the other day. I reckon that between us we must know something like four or five thousand tunes. Some of them you don't realise you know, until somebody plays them and you suddenly find yourself playing along with them. I think Aly's the same as me. He learns by osmosis a lot of the time. You know, he hears a tune and it just kind of seeps into him. I remember once I had written a tune but never actively rehearsed it. I started playing it during a sound-check, and the next thing I knew, Aly was playing it with me, note for note. Traditional musicians have a better ear than classical musicians because they don't rely on written music. I think Aly has a highly developed version of that, just as some people have a wee bit ESP and others have got loads. Aly's ear has been fine-tuned, out of necessity. When you know so many tunes, you begin to recognise the form. So Violet Tulloch can accompany a tune without ever having heard it before – unless you toss in a bender that's going to throw her. But nine times out of ten, the chord changes will follow.

We first got together in 1986, for the pilot series of *Aly Bain and Friends*, when it was Aly, Violet, Mary Black, Dick Gaughan and myself. It seemed to go down well, and when Aly did the next series, he included me. We kind of cemented a friendship early on when we were doing a thing for Alister Anderson in the Queen Elizabeth Hall in London. Aly asked me out for an Italian meal one night, and he basically said he was sorry he had been such a shit to me for so long. I had no idea what he was talking about, although I knew he used to give me a row for playing a tune a certain way. He said he didn't know why he had done that, and he really respected what I did as a musician. I remember thinking at the time, well, that's a really nice thing for someone to do, because if you yourself have made a mistake it's very difficult to admit it. I thought the guy had a lot going for him.

Nowadays, we have arguments from time to time when we're on the road, usually

At the recording session for Scottish Television's Aly Bain and Friends *(1987) at the Riverside, Glasgow, with Violet Tulloch, Phil Cunningham and Willie Johnson*

late at night, and when Aly comes out with 'Du doesn't ken thee as well as I kens thee', then I know it's my cue to go to bed. But most of the time, touring with Aly is a gas. If a psychiatrist was to sit behind us in the Volvo, he could write volumes on us. We have a crazy time. We never speak in our own voices – it's aye like Robbie Shepherd, or someone like that [Phil and Aly, like so many 'ear' musicians, are brilliantly wicked mimics]. When I get home, my wife asks me a question and I'll reply in Aly's voice: 'Whit does du ken about onything?' Aly's favourite pastime in the car would interest the psychiatrist. He's always looking out for good places for an ambush. Every time we go round a corner in the Highlands, he'll say: 'You could have a fine ambush here.'

After *Aly Bain and Friends*, my musical involvement with Aly got bigger and bigger. The response to the telly series was so good that we thought we should try a tour. It was only a short thing, just eleven dates, a few gigs in Scotland and a weekend in Denmark. It was a great change for me after all those years in the band, sitting on the edge of your seat squeezing as hard as you can, pumping out as much energy as you could. I suddenly discovered with Aly that I could get through a whole gambit of really relaxed music and just drop in the flashy stuff now and again – for the sake of proving I could still do it! With Aly, you sit back in your chair and play tunes that you really enjoy at a pace you enjoy playing them. It kind of calmed me down after all the frantic years. We began playing a lot of tunes I'd always liked but never had an opportunity to play. Silly Wizard and Relativity were all about power in terms of instrumentals. There was no relaxed instrumental in the whole history of Silly Wizard – we were all blasting it out.

Playing with Aly inspired my air composing, because there's nothing better than to write a slow air that you would normally play on the box and to hear somebody like Aly playing it. I've written more airs in the time I've been with Aly than I've ever written. Sometimes we'll be just messing about, and I'll say: 'Try this line.' And he'll play a line, and out of it a whole air will appear, because the way he plays it is the way I hear it in my head. I can never make that sound on the box. So as a compositional tool, he's great!

Mind you, we still play helluva fast, which a lot of people don't like. And after every fast piece we end up debating as to which of the two of us speeded up. 'Du played too fast for me,' he'll say. 'It was you, Aly,' I'll tell him. 'It was not me,' he'll reply, and so on.

It's kind of weird, but the accordion has been an incredible bind in my life. It was the thing I was good at doing, and when I found myself in the position of being a professional musician, that was what I was playing. But I've never really liked it. Now that I'm playing with Aly, I like the box a lot better because it fits in with what we're doing. I've always dabbled in keyboards and been trying to improve what I'm doing. When I'm at home, all the music I write for films or documentaries is keyboard-based. But I don't do much piano with Aly. I've got this left hand on my box all fixed so that I can trigger electronic keyboards from it.

Aly hates going out on stage on his own. I think you could walk out there and sit beside him and not play a note, and he'd get on fine, because he's so good at drawing the whole audience in to what he's doing. He just wants somebody there with him, in case he rips his breeks or something. But he's beautiful to play with, and for me the annual tour is something I always look forward to. It's incredibly civilised. We sit on the ferry to Stornoway and play bridge, would you believe! And because all our concerts are sold out, the money is good and we stay in really good hotels. It's nice, easy touring – magic.

The concert I remember best was at the Eden Court Theatre in January 1993. Violet came down from Shetland, and we had two days in my house at Beauly. Generally, we only met up a few hours before the gig, and this was the first opportunity we'd ever had to spend time working things out as a trio. So we were in pretty good nick by the time we got to Inverness. The atmosphere in the hall was great, and it went like a dream. Everything was spot-on – you know, all the changes. And because we had played a lot in the previous September we had kind of remembered all the wee connecting things that the other person was doing. It was quite funny, because Aly and I would find ourselves both going for the same harmonies – so there would be no tune left. But that's the nice thing about it. Because it's a fairly simple approach to what we're doing we don't have to rehearse that much. It takes one or two gigs to kind of sink back with each other again.

I'd been wondering what would happen at that Eden Court concert, because of the previous time we played there. Aly had been trying out a couple of tunes in the house the day before, *The Auld Fiddler* and a tune we called *The Bastard in B-flat* because we don't know what it's called and it's a very awkward tune for both the fiddle and the box. At the end of the concert, we got an encore and, as Aly is occasionally prone to do, he changed his mind about what we would play, and he sprang this set on me out of nowhere.

I had only played the tunes maybe twice in my life. I didn't really know them. He just said: 'Yes, that's what we're going to play.' An argument started on stage, and at one point I turned to the audience and said: 'Don't go away, we'll be with you soon.' Eventually I gave in, and we launched into this thing. The minute we started, Aly realised that we didn't know it. But we were committed. We were both bug-eyed as we played – sheer panic on my face and his. When we finished, the sweat was just blinding us. Violet was behind us, in stitches of laughter, because she only had the chords to play. The audience didn't seem to mind. They loved it.

What I like about Aly's playing is the wide spectrum he can cover in terms of style. And he can sometimes draw a thing from one area that he's very familiar with and drop it into another. So you'll hear wee Texas influences coming in when he plays Scottish waltzes – just the way he phrases certain notes. He's so widely travelled that he has tune sources from everywhere – Finland, Norway, Louisiana, Russia and so on. So he's an incredibly versatile player, which makes him good for doing gigs with because you're not stuck in the same thread all the way through. And at the risk of being lynched by all the other fiddlers on the planet, I'd say that I've never heard anybody play a slow air like him. He has an incredible tone and an incredible feel for a slow air.

DAVE RICHARDSON

Since 1979, when Robin Morton left the Boys of the Lough, Dave Richardson has doubled as musician and band manager, handling all the business from his home in Edinburgh. Strictly speaking, he's the only Englishman in the band. Less strictly, he's regarded as more or less Scottish on the grounds that he's a Geordie, born just south of the Border. He came into the band as a temporary replacement for Dick Gaughan at a time when he was heading for a PhD in molecular biology. One trip to the States was all that was needed to persuade him to abandon his studies . . .

They phoned me at one in the morning to say that they wanted me for a tour for three weeks in the States. I borrowed the money from my mother for the flight. It was about £80. That was an awful lot of money at the time. It could buy you 640 pints of beer — there were eight to the pound. The first gig was in Mount Clare College in New Jersey. Before we flew from Shannon Airport we went to the duty free and bought fifteen quarts of whisky and 3,000 cigarettes because that was the time when Aly was getting married to Lucy and he needed all these supplies. Lucy's mother just about had a fit when she saw all the booze. She thought: what's my daughter marrying?

That tour was a success. I came home with as much money in my pocket as I'd had to live on all year as student, so I was thrilled. I was doing a post-graduate certificate in education. I didn't really think I'd be a teacher, but I thought it would buy me time to finish my PhD. I did finish the teaching course, but in the summer we spent ten weeks in the States, and when I came back I just knew that I was never going back to the lab. After the American tour, there had to be a decision. The band was getting so much work. We were playing at weekends and staying with people. You were always somebody's guest. It was like one long party. There was no thought of work or professionalism or being organised. It was pretty chaotic. But it was such an exciting alternative to what I was doing, and more and more the idea of working as a biologist became a big pain.

On those first gigs in the States we played in dry venues. After doing all these folk clubs in Britain, which were basically pubs and where the musicians were drinking as well as everybody else, we found ourselves playing in coffee-houses where you couldn't even get a beer on a hot day. So you then started to focus on *why* you were there. You were there to perform, deliver a product, rather than to be part of a party. So our attitude as musicians started to change.

But, looking back, it was a wild time. We stayed up late, went to parties, didn't get enough sleep. We always set off late for the gig. The speed limit then was 75, and we always did over 90, so we were always getting speeding tickets, and when the police stopped us we had to hide the beer we had been drinking in the car.

It was pretty clear on those first trips that this was instrumental music taking off. Americans were already listening to their own string-band music. When we went to those festivals on the east coast there were old-timey bands with a couple of fiddles, string bass, banjo and guitar. So our music just went right in on top of that, with the added attraction that we could offer woodwind (the flute) and reeds (the concertina).

So the Americans were interested in our instrumental thing, the technique thing. And, of course, when they heard Aly and Cathal for the first time, they came back again. We were also young and iconoclastic. It's hard for people to believe now, but we were like the Pogues in a way, on stage with our drinks and just being generally disrespectful. Then we moved out of the coffee-houses. You wouldn't take drink on stage in a concert hall. Also, you wouldn't get hired if you appeared in the clothes you had been travelling in. So we smartened up our act a bit.

At the same time, there was a massive end to the swinging '60s, and things became very conservative in America. Nowadays, there's no sense of people getting wild as there used to be. We are travelling less and doing better work now, and that's much better for the health. It's more selective now, and the guys in the band have been able to do other projects. We haven't had road-burn for years. I used to keep a diary on those first American tours, and every second entry says: 'Everyone totally exhausted.'

It's a very different scene now. Twenty years ago, there was only a limited number of festivals and a limited number of venues. We worked really hard. We had some appalling tours, the sort of conditions where you're doing long journeys and not getting much money for it – paying your dues. We used to feel much more competitive then, especially if some new band came along and got the headline spot in a festival which you thought was yours. But the scene is so vigorous now. Even if there were no other bands competing against you, you still couldn't do the work. It's very healthy to have all the diversity. I don't mind if a band comes along and presents the music in a different way. That's how it should be, otherwise we'd all be clones.

It's hard to tell what people want. You think you're going out there to play music, but you're not only doing that. There's something else that people seem to be wanting. When a band like the Dubliners started up, the big attraction was that they were big and hairy, drank Guinness on stage, and looked definitely counter-establishment. And all the blue-collar people who had been screwed down for years and years thought this was great because their own attitudes were suddenly getting centre-stage. When it comes to Americans, they have this dream image of Scotland and the Celtic world, and you go on stage and somehow you fulfil it. And yet it's the last thing in your head; you're not even thinking about it.

Aly has very high standards musically. He won't just play anything, unless it's got far into the night and he's had a lot to drink. His television work has raised the band's profile, although in the beginning you get paranoia in a band whenever anybody starts doing something different because you think: is he leaving the ship? And there have been occasional problems when people have seen Aly getting separate billing outside the Boys of the Lough and have come to the conclusion that he has left the band.

When it comes to the actual playing, he is quite clearly the leader of the band. He establishes the beat and we play to him, no question. When it comes to repertoire, Cathal plays an influential role. But when it comes to performance, if anything goes wrong with Aly it's like the keystone comes out of the arch. He has this massive physical strength, which you need for the fiddle. His physical power is important. Carignon was like that – barrel-chested, strong. Also, Aly is extremely well coordinated. He was a fine badminton player in his youth, and he has this athleticism which I think is a key to the way he plays. There's just no physical problem at all. And he has a great ear. He and Phil Cunningham are the only guys I know who can imitate Kevin Burke's accent – an Irish one with a London Cockney component. And it's this incredible ability to reproduce something accurately which is the sign of a good ear.

On top of all that, there's just not that many people who can actually play some of the repertoire Aly plays. Probably Alistair Fraser can do it. But a lot of Scottish fiddle music is a paradox. It's just not available to a lot of players because it's so hard. All the Skinner stuff – all the virtuoso stuff – has ruined it for a lot of vernacular players.

Aly's attitude to rival fiddlers – and there's plenty of them around these days – has changed. There was a time when he was Billy the Kid – if another gunslinger came into the bar, that guy had to be killed! When we got him and Frankie Gavin together, it was just immediate. Gavin would come out with the fast Galway tunes that Aly wouldn't know, and Aly would say: 'Oh, that's very good,' and then Aly would slip into the flat keys, like B-flat and E-flat, which Frankie couldn't handle at that time. That created a definite edge to the music – here was another fiddler, and he had to be shown who was boss. Aly doesn't seem to have to feel he has to prove that now.

The biggest thing that Aly's done for the fiddle is making it sound really beautiful and good. There are so many horrible players who have no tone or anything – it's just a rasp, and sometimes there's no tune. And people think: oh God, that's the tradition, is it? Whereas he's right on top of it technically. He's got vibrato, an ability to produce that great tone. It's a sound that people want to listen to.

CATHAL McCONNELL

Cathal comes from Country Fermanagh, in Northern Ireland, and belongs to a family that has a long pedigree in traditional music. At the tender age of thirteen he had shouldered aside the older players and taken the all-Ireland championship titles in both flute and whistle. By the time he helped to form the Boys of the Lough, he was in his mid-twenties, but apart from a few tours as a duo with Robin Morton, he had seen very little of the world. 'When I first met Cathal,' says Aly, 'he was very naïve – just the way I was when I left Shetland. He couldn't really deal with life outside Ireland at first. Robin took care of everything, so really all that Cathal had to do was to follow Robin around everywhere and appear on stage at night. In the early days, he was so engrossed in the music that he never really knew where we were, or where we were going next day. I remember once we left New York and we drove through New Jersey and Pennsylvania and we were into Ohio – twelve hours down the road – when Cathal said, "New York's a really big place, isn't it?" And quite often on stage he would say to the audience: "Well, it's great to be here in . . ." and turn round to Dave and say: "Where are we?" Nowadays, he plays at being a lot more naïve than he is – so that we'll do everything for him!'

Cathal's air of naïveté has unintentionally evolved into an integral part of any Boys of the Lough concert. In particular, he likes to make friends with the audience, and he will sit and blether to them for ages in a delightful, rambling, stream-of-consciousness way that has brought smiles to the most stony-faced of audiences. It tends to relax the band, too. During the 1970s, they appeared for the first time at the prestigious Usher Hall in Edinburgh. The 2,000-capacity house was full, and all of the Boys, including Cathal, were extremely nervous.

'There was whisky backstage,' Cathal recalls. 'So I had a few drinks, although I wasn't drunk. I was introducing the band, and I said something like: "Good evening, ladies and gentlemen. I'm delighted to be here, and I don't mind telling you I'm a bit nervous tonight, so I had a few drinks before I came on stage." And the audience just cracked up! They had never heard this kind of thing before. From then on, the night was won – just by me saying the wrong thing.'

I'll vouch for that. I was in the audience that night, and I think it was on that occasion that Cathal came out with: 'This tune's in E-flat. Which is a different key from D, and, of course, also different from B-flat.' And so it went on, sentence after sentence of tortuously simplistic but irrefutable truth.

'He can say the simplest thing,' says Dave Richardson, 'and everybody falls about. There's definitely a persona there that people like and can relate to. When Cathal's having one of his strangely quiet nights the rest of us have to work much harder.'

Aly says: 'He's a great guy to have on stage because, apart from being a wonderful musician, he breaks down an audience. People don't understand how important that is. He's just got a way with him. People feel they want to help him out, and he knows that. What actually happens is that he begins speaking before he knows what he's going to say, so whatever comes out, comes out. I remember we played one night in Melbourne and he set off on one of his spiels, and he kept getting himself into things he hadn't thought about, so he was going through this verbal maze. And the audience were helpless with laughter. We actually went off the stage and left him to talk. The Australians loved it, and after that the whole night came to life.'

Cathal himself thinks that he picked up this gift for genial blarney from a couple of Irish musicians who were also great storytellers, Micky and Johnny Doherty. 'They were marvellous at introducing tunes. The McConnell family are all a bit long-winded and we tend to meander. I think there is that part in us naturally. We have a lot of information about tunes and about people and we want to put this across to the audience, but sometimes it doesn't come out the way I intend it to.'

'He loves to perform,' says Aly. 'He hardly speaks to anyone until about half past five at night. And then he gets up on stage and talks the whole evening.'

Cathal argues that the Boys of the Lough's set-up on stage, with five musicians on chairs, concentrating on their music with very little movement for the audience to watch, means that 'you have to be entertaining on stage as a person'. He goes on: 'Sometimes the music isn't quite enough.'

Cathal first heard Aly playing with Mike Whellans at a festival in Aberdeen. 'I knew I was listening to a great player. I played with Aly socially afterwards, and I was very impressed by what he was doing. We had a friend in common, Sean Maguire, who was a Northern Irish fiddle player interested in Scottish music, and I knew a lot of his repertoire. It turned out that Aly knew a lot of his records, too. Music in the north of Ireland is fairly similar to a lot of Scottish music. When you go down to Clare, say, the music becomes different, more relaxed. Aly was more like the Donegal or Antrim style of fiddle. He has a very definite idea about Irish music and what he likes and doesn't like. I had heard some Scottish music, but I had never heard Shetland music before I heard Aly – never. He was the first man to bring it to Ireland.'

Somehow, Cathal and Aly found a common musical language almost instantly, and their mutual respect shows through in everything they play together.

'He's a great musician,' says Aly, 'but he's not the kind of guy who would ever tell anybody that or take any credit for it. He really comes up with more ideas than anyone else in the band, and more arrangements and harmonies – all that kind of stuff, a lot of it comes from him. He's also got a great love for music, and picks really good tunes and songs. He's a great player to work with. He does harmonies on the spot and he does things on stage that are really daring. He's not frightened to try something, and he's prepared to learn from his mistakes.'

Music so dominates Cathal's life that it's hard sometimes to get him to stop making it. Aly recalls one American tour when the band got so fed up with the incessant sound of Cathal on the road that they banned him from playing the flute in the car. So Cathal put his flute away and then decided to fill the time by writing down the words of every song that he knew. The Boys thought this was a splendid idea: it would keep him occupied and give them some peace and quiet. They bought him a thick exercise book, and Cathal got to work. The trouble was, of course, that Cathal couldn't write down the words without singing them at the same time, or playing a tape to remind himself how the words went. The singing and humming were not quite so distracting as the flute, however, so the Boys let him get on with it. Cathal filled the exercise book. In its finished state, it stood as a valuable folksong collection that could well have found its way into one of the great archives. A few days before the end of the tour, Cathal laid his treasure down somewhere and lost it. He was so crestfallen, they let him play the flute in the car.

WILLIE JOHNSON

It's perhaps odd that a guitarist should be part of the triumvirate that shaped the modern sound of Shetland fiddling, but 'Peerie' Willie Johnson played a crucial part, along with Tom Anderson and Aly Bain. It was Willie who put swing into Shetland music. It was Willie who introduced the intriguing chord patterns that most Shetland accompanists now use. Basically, it all come from his first love, jazz. As a youngster his great inspiration was the American guitarist Eddie Lang, who played with the jazz fiddler Joe Venuti. Willie and Tom heard this music during the 1930s on short-wave radio and on the records that merchant seamen brought back to Shetland. Many years

With Tom and Willie at Schenectady, New York State (1979). It was a great thrill for Tom and Willie to find themselves on the same stage from which Joe Venuti and Eddie Lang had broadcast some forty years earlier

later, in 1979, when they joined the Boys of the Lough for an American tour, they had the thrill of playing in the very hall, at Schenectady, from which the Lang-Venuti sessions had been broadcast.

'It was Willie who took Eddie Lang's chords and his own chords and put them to fiddle music,' says Aly. 'And, of course, they fitted perfectly. And it's the same rhythm that we have now on piano – we call it "dumchik'" because that's the way the rhythm goes. Willie had a genius for working out chords. In fact, he figured them all out on piano first and then transposed the chords to the guitar. He introduced tenths, ninths, thirteenths and flattened fifths – all the things that the jazzmen were playing – and he passed it on to the next generation of Shetland pianists, Ronnie Cooper and Violet Tulloch, because they worked with Willie in various bands after the war.

Willie's adventurous chord sequences didn't always find favour with Tom Anderson. As Willie puts it: 'I had to keep it very basic at first with Tom, nothing fancy, because he wanted it that way. In any case, you can't put a lot of thirteenths and flattened fifths into Shetland reels – it takes away from it, in my opinion. You try to keep it the way it's supposed to be, and that's the way Tom liked it. But later on, especially when we went to America, I started doing a lot of flattened-fifth things and Tom came round eventually.

'The whole art of accompaniment, whether you're playing for a singer or a fiddler, is that you don't want to fancy it up, because it detracts from the soloist. I always play a shade behind the soloist, not the same level. You musn't overshadow the soloist, fly all over the place.

'There was nobody really playing here in Shetland when I started. I had to teach myself. Nowadays, people ask me about chords, and I tell them they have to figure it out for themselves. When Tommy taught his pupils, everything had to be correct, the way he played it. I like to encourage them to play something different, so I try to put them on the road and give them the basics, and then they can take off on their own from there.'

That, roughly, is the way that Aly learned from Willie in his formative fiddling years, and it was Willie's playing, and Willie's record collection, that planted the seeds of his love for jazz and American fiddle music.

Willie can well remember the first time he set eyes on Aly Bain. 'I was up at Tom's house having a tune. The front door was open, so I got up to close it, and Tom said: "Leave it open, Willie. The peerie boy from next door likes to come in and hear the fiddle." This is Aly. He was just a wee bairn. Sure enough, we're playing away and he comes crawling in and just sat in front of Tommy, watching him playing, with his mouth wide open. And then his mother came in and took him away to his bed.'

Over the years, a great musical friendship developed, largely through the mutual relationship with Tom Anderson. Aly has never lost faith in the guitarist, with whom he has toured and recorded extensively. Even today, in his seventies, Willie Johnson will pick up his telephone and find Aly at the other end of the line, asking him to catch the plane for a TV show or a concert.

'That's one of the great things about Aly,' he says. 'He's given Shetland musicians exposure. And by his own example he's encouraged Shetlanders not to be so inward-looking. Shetlanders never used to want to go to the mainland. They didn't want to try anything new. But Aly has encouraged them to go, and he has given them their chance on television.

'There's hundreds of good fiddlers on the islands now. I heard a wee kid the other day playing *The High Level*, and that used to be a real test piece. If you could play it, you were a good player. And this wee kid just rattled it off no bother at all.'

Willie's only regret about the new generation of fiddle wizards is that they tend to play 'at a hell of a speed'. He makes the fascinating point that in the old days, when coal was an expensive luxury on the islands, and long before the arrival of central heating, the fiddlers were inhibited to some extent by the heavy layers of clothing that they had to wear.

'I played with a lot of the old Shetland fiddlers, donkey's years ago, and it was all Shetland style. But it was slower than they play it now. That's how they got the lift in their playing – and that's what's gone now. Very few fiddlers do it now. Aly does it, and Willie Hunter and Davy Tulloch. That slower stuff was what Tommy was trying to collect. It's just a different style. I used to play the guitar fast, but you can't get the lift if you play too fast. Aly can do it when there's speed, you see. He's got it kind of perfected that he can play all these things and get the tone and the lift when there's speed. He kind of digs into it. He's aye got the life. A lot of fiddlers play it pretty straight, to the book, no matter how good a tone they've got. Aly's got more life in it, and that counts a lot when you're playing reels and things like that.'

Willie warns, too, of the effect on young players, especially guitarists, of the electronic revolution. 'Electronics have ruined playing in a lot of ways. Electric guitar is kind of easy, you don't have to work at it. You just tinkle the thing and you've got the tone.'

The 1979 American tour that Willie and Tom took with the Boys of the Lough was a punishing one in terms of travelling. It stretched from Alaska in the north to San Francisco in the south. Tom was in his mid-sixties by then. Aly, wondering if the old boy would stand up to strain, was relieved to hear Tom say that he wasn't going to drink on the tour – only soft drinks. 'The soft drinks turned out to be gin and tonics,' says Aly. 'During the tour, he kept saying he thought he had ulcers, but the problem was the amount of gin that was going through his body. He actually finished the tour in better shape than any of us. He could have done another one. We were all knackered.'

There had always been a history of love-hate friction and rivalry between Willie and Tom. Aly used to regard them as Laurel and Hardy, with Tom playing the dominant role, and the gin and tonics only served to exacerbate the situation. 'No matter what Willie said, Tom would have to equal it, or better it,' says Aly. 'When we went to San Francisco, Tom had some cousin who wanted to take him out to see the Redwoods. So off Tom went one day, and we were relieved, because you couldn't really relax when he was around. We wanted to see the Redwoods too, so we took Willie along with us. We got back at night, and Willie said to Tom: "By Christ, Tammy, I saw the Redwoods today. Christ, du's never seen trees dat size. You could drive a car through the middle of them." Tom, who was a huge man, drew himself up to his full height and said: "Redwoods! What the f–ing hell docs du know about Redwoods? My cousin has lived here all his life, and I saw far bigger Redwoods than du ever saw!"'

On stage the next night, Tom and Willie played together like angels.

In Alaska, the Boys played in one of the roughest joints they have ever played in, the Crystal Saloon in Juneau. The customers came in carrying guns, and it was like a scene from the Wild West. The couple who ran the bar collapsed in a drunken heap at one point, and Aly and Willie had to act as bartenders. For amusement, the Alaskans would fire a shotgun into an empty oil drum and listen to the shot ricocheting round the drum. 'It was really wild,' says Aly. 'I was worried about how Tom would take it all, but he was in his element. He loved it. He said it felt just like Shetland.'

Willie Johnson proved a hit with the Alaskans, just as he had everywhere else on that tour, although there was never a realistic prospect of his becoming a full-time Boy of the Lough. There was an occasion later, however, when it seemed for a brief, inebriated moment, that Aly was contemplating putting his musical partnership with the guitarist on a permanent basis. Owen Hand tells the lovely story of how they were all in the bar after a concert and Aly was down in the dumps for some reason and feeling that it was maybe time for the Boys of the Lough to call it a day. 'Some drink had been taken,' says Owen. 'Aly and I were having a chat, and Aly suddenly said he was thinking of quitting the band and "going back to play with old Willie". Then a wee frown came over his face and he went over to Willie and said: "Willie, how long does du think du'll live for?"'

Happily, Willie is very much alive and well and still playing fine guitar.

VIOLET TULLOCH

As a teenager in Shetland, Aly Bain would see a beautiful girl playing accordion with Tom Anderson's Isleburgh band. 'She was so beautiful, any man would have died over her,' says Aly. But Violet Tulloch was not just the proverbial pretty face. She was also a highly talented player with a superbly fluent sense of rhythm, and hearing Violet was one of the things that spurred Aly to work harder on the fiddle. 'It wasn't so much that I fancied her – which I did! It was that I couldn't wait to be able to do the things that she was doing with the music. I thought to myself: how can I impress her, how can I learn more than she's learned?' Today, Violet remains Aly's favourite accompanist and she has joined him on records, television and concert gigs. 'Through her accompaniment,' he says, 'she opened my ears to the art of slow air playing. We work a great deal together, and her advice and playing have given me a deeper understanding of the music I play. She and her husband Drew are among my dearest friends.'

I think the first time I met Aly was in a house in the next street one New Year's Eve. Drew, my husband, and I had gone visiting these folk, and this young fiddler came in. I think he must have been about sixteen or seventeen, and I had the accordion with me and we just got going and we seemed to relate right from the word go. I thought then this boy is really going to be something else. There was great fire in his playing at that time, slightly intense, but you always knew that this was something special coming out.

Like many fiddlers in those days he had come across an LP of Sean Maguire, and he was really into it. I'm sure he would admit himself that this was one LP where he knew every track on it. He sat hour after hour until he got the lot, and probably as a result of the technique that Sean Maguire used on *The Mason's Apron*, Aly picked up on that and started playing around the tune, and then everybody was trying to do this style.

One of the things I really like about Aly and will always appreciate is that he never allows the music to become too narrow. You can hear him playing Shetland reels, and he's carried that to every corner of the world, his own traditional music. But you can hear him playing the old Bill Hardie style, the Methlick style, one week – and then the next week you'll find that he's jetting across to America to appear on somebody's album over there. I think *Down Home* speaks for that. The incredible thing is that when he adopts the different styles, you could swear that Aly had been born among the Cape Bretons, or whatever. It's this amazing openness about him – he seems able to cope with anything that's thrown at him.

Aly's slow airs were weak at one time. He wanted to play fast, and at that time there were a lot of fiddlers in that school of thought. But I think he came to realise that you lost a lot of the notes playing so fast. Nowadays, if you were speaking to the Willie Hunters of this world they'd agree that Aly has got his playing under control.

Mind you, the wildness is still in there and he still takes me by surprise. You can think you're going to do a march, strathspey and reel, in whatever order, and all of a sudden he just does something else, and I don't know what has happened inside him, but out it comes. And it's really nice. Because if it happens to him, it happens to me. I think that's the thing about Aly and me – we both think the same about music. He knows that I love slow airs, and he certainly loves them, and maybe it's because we're both emotional people.

I love playing with him and Phil Cunningham, because there again I get the chance to sort of expand what I'm doing, get away from Shetland reels. Because of the geographical problem, we can't get together often. If we're playing in Shetland, Aly and Phil will arrive here at 2 p.m. on the day of the concert, and you've just got that three hours in the afternoon before you go on stage. But that gets easier because we've played a long time together.

Shetland fiddlers have always been spoilt for good accompaniment. The late Ronnie Cooper was one of Aly's favourites. Every fiddler has had a reasonable backing, so none of them want to go on stage and play unaccompanied fiddle. That's never been a Shetland thing. If you did it at a concert, you'd find that Shetlanders would just switch off – they're so used to hearing something going on behind the fiddler. God knows, Aly has had to play with some terrible accompanists in his time, but he always likes to have one there.

A lot of electric keyboards are on the go now in Shetland. A lot of the village halls didn't maintain their pianos, and so they threw them out. So bands started carrying their own small keyboards, and I don't like them. I've tried them – I'll play anything with notes on it! But you'll never get a good slow air from an electric keyboard.

But generally the music in Shetland has opened up a lot more. Aly has been a great influence on the kids. I accompanied a young boy on fiddle the other week, Brian Gair. He's a fine player, and I could tell that he obviously hero-worships Aly. Everywhere I go playing around Shetland, the kids are into Aly Bain, and it's good that I'm here to keep an eye on them, because when I'm playing with them and they get a note wrong I can say: change that note. You don't want to interfere with their style of playing, but they must get the notes right.

Aly is a pleasure to play with, and he's done really well. Folk here appreciate the hard struggle that he had in the early years, and it's nice to see him getting the reward for that.

ALY BAIN

MALCOLM GREEN

As chief executive of Shetland Islands Council, Malcolm Green has helped to steer the islands through the boom years of the North Sea oil industry, and he became a familiar face on national television when the tanker Braer *came to grief in January 1993, spilling thousands of gallons of oil into the precious Shetland waters that provide such an important prop to the local economy. He is a quiet, reticent Englishman with a greying beard, who radiates a sense of calm before any storm. This is a prerequisite for the job, for he occupies a hot seat, and nothing he could ever do would please all of the Shetlanders all of the time. The long, twisting trail that took him to Shetland from Derbyshire and a career with the* Guardian *newspaper began with fiddle music . . .*

It all started in 1978, when I saw there was a fiddle course at the summer school at Stirling University, and Aly Bain was advertised as one of the tutors. I knew Aly's name from the Boys of the Lough. I didn't know anything about Shetland or Shetland music. So I went up to Stirling for the course in July, and it turned out that Aly wasn't the tutor, it was Tom Anderson. It was a great week. When I left Stirling, I was very close to tears. It really was one of the best things in my life.

Up till then, my interest had been largely the English end of things – people like Dave Swarbrick. My father, who was a good classical violinist, had left me his fiddle and I had never learned to play it properly; I felt I had let my father down.

Soon after Stirling, I did meet Aly Bain. He came down to England on tour with Tom Anderson and they came to Derbyshire and I went to see them. We all went back to the house and the guy I was with had two bottles of whisky. I remember listening to Aly playing slow airs, although he wasn't really in a state to play them properly.

All of this had made me want to learn more about the fiddle and more about Shetland. It just so happened that in August of that year there was a job advertised in Shetland. It was in the finance department. It wouldn't have meant anything to me if I hadn't seen Aly's name as the tutor on the fiddle course, and gone to Stirling and met Tom Anderson. I came up to Shetland in September for an interview, got the job, and moved up in December. It all happened very fast.

When I came here I started to play with the Forty Fiddlers, but shortly afterwards Tom left the Fiddlers. He asked me early on to go to the inaugural meeting for the Shetland Folk Festival. They elected me as their first chairman, and I've been here ever since. So I got involved in the music side as both an organiser and a musician. Dave Swarbrick sent an invitation for the Forty Fiddlers to go down and play at the Fairport Convention reunion. The Fiddlers couldn't do it, so I put my own band together. I took three fiddlers, an electric guitar, electric bass and keyboard and we called it Garston's Dream Band. We had a great time and we played for an audience of about 10,000. So, musically, I had done what I wanted to do.

I didn't get instruction from Aly. My fiddling, apart from Stirling, has been self-taught. I'm fairly shy about it, to be honest. To come here as an Englishman and play the fiddle was a bit cheeky.

I don't think what Aly has done has been properly recognised here. The kind of music he played – still plays – is minority music, but he is starting to develop into a popular entertainer in lots of ways and has become a good ambassador for Shetland, in all its aspects, not just the music. For example, he's very committed to the concept of the marine environment, very keen to see Shetland look after itself, very passionate about Shetland.

I think what Aly did was unique, and is still unique because he's still building his reputation: he's the only one that's gone and earned a living with his music. I don't think a lot of people understand the pain that goes into building that kind of career and reputation – it's a building job. It's Aly more than Tom Anderson who has taken Shetland music out into the world. Aly pioneered the road to America.

Tom's great pioneering role was to start all the teaching here. Today the fiddle is taught inside the schools and outside the schools, and you have people like Willie Hunter who's got ninety pupils. Tom was teaching ninety before he died. And other teachers like Trevor Hunter, Margaret Robertson, Eunice Henderson – they've all got lots of pupils. And some of the youngsters coming up are frighteningly talented. You can recognise each teacher when the pupils play – whether it's Willie Hunter or whoever – but at the same time the pupils all have their personal qualities.

Shetland needs Aly Bain. What the *Braer* tanker has done is to damage Shetland, violate it, and it has left an image in people's minds, the image of oil, filth, people struggling, and things dying. Television has all its archive footage of the *Braer*. It's what they show when they're talking about Shetland.

So we need to re-market Shetland. You've got to push into people's homes a picture of Shetland that's clean, inviolable, where the products are clean and worth buying. And you can't do that with a TV travelogue, because people won't watch it. But you can do it through music, through entertainment. You need to pull in musicians who are internationally famous, and almost by the way say this place is clean. So you need Aly for that. You need to use his contacts, like Billy Connolly – people who care about a place like this. So the whole thing is circular. Aly to a large extent needs Shetland as his base, to draw from it the things that he needs. And Shetland needs him.

Chapter Seven

WALTZING WITH ALY

When I first heard that Aly Bain had agreed to play in concert with the classical violinist Leonard Friedman, I could hardly believe my ears. Not because I thought Aly might come a cropper in such exalted company – although that was a distinct possibility, as he hadn't played a note of classical music since his boyhood – but because I knew that for many years he had nursed a wee grievance against the academic musical establishment. It went back to the time when he was fourteen years old and was persuaded by Tom Anderson to enter a competition at the Shetland Music Festival. The competitors had to play two short classical pieces, followed by a fiddle tune. The prize was a superb £200 violin, which actually belonged to an elderly relative of Aly.

Aly wanted that fiddle, and he wanted to win that competition. At home, he diligently played the music over and over again. It was one of the few occasions in his musical lifetime that he practised for a public performance. When the great day arrived and he stood up to play, he managed to get through the musical assault course in reasonable shape, despite a severe attack of nerves. The adjudicator, a classical teacher from Aberdeen, was certainly impressed, and awarded Aly the top marks. That should have been the end of it, but it wasn't. As Aly recalls: 'After much mumbling in the corner it was announced that, even though I had won, the prize would go to the player who was second because he was going on to high school and probably university and would make better use of the instrument than I would, as I was leaving school at fifteen.'

There was uproar in the hall. 'Tom Anderson blew a fuse and my brother, who was home from university, complained to the adjudicator. Eventually, in order to justify their decision, they gave us both a music-reading test, which, of course, my opponent won – mainly because I couldn't read music! I went home feeling numb. I have never forgotten the injustice done to me that day. I still feel angry whenever I think about it. My opponent's father had an important job, with influence. We were just ordinary people. It was a class snob thing.'

The incident never soured Aly's appreciation of classical music itself. While he would think twice about crossing the road to hear a violin concerto, he often enjoys good classical music when it's thrust upon him – perhaps at the homes of his 'Lost Patrol' Edinburgh buddies, Alan Rankin and Carl Pidgeon, who both take fiendish delight in reaching for their Bartóks the moment he opens the door. But, understandably, the Lerwick violin competition left him with a deep suspicion of the people who wield power in music's orthodox church.

So the Leonard Friedman concert, in July 1992, came as a surprise even to those who recognised Aly as an incurable musical maverick. It was held as part of the Stockbridge Festival in Edinburgh, in a hall not far from Aly's home in the Colonies. Once again, Aly had to sit down at home and practise. This time it was a Bach piece, which had to dovetail precisely (as classical things do) into another Bach composition played by Leonard.

Technically, there was no problem for Aly in learning the Bach music from a cassette that Leonard had given him. But, on the night, that faithful, highly receptive Bain ear, which for thirty years had been trained to pick up tunes and store them in the memory bank, almost brought about a professionally embarrassing calamity.

Leonard played his melody first as a solo. Standing there, listening to the maestro, Aly – who was not, of course, using sheet music – got so hooked on the smoothly flowing Bach tones that when the time came for him to start playing, he discovered to his horror that his own part had gone clean out of his head. All he could think of was the music that Leonard was performing. So that's what Aly began to play – which in itself was a remarkable achievement, as he had never learned Leonard's part. After several bars, with both musicians playing the same notes, Aly's part suddenly came back to him, and he was able to provide the contrapuntal line that Leonard had been anticipating. Happily, the whole thing worked amazingly well and none of the critics spotted the impromptu rearrangement. Aly's slight discomfiture in classical mode was mirrored by Leonard's later difficulties with the rhythms of a Shetland reel, so honours at the end of the evening were more or less shared. Leonard Friedman was clearly thrilled by the occasion, and vowed to repeat it, which the two musicians did in a 1993 recital.

Would Aly have made a great classical violinist if he had been awarded that competition prize in Shetland, had been put through a conservatoire training and had been taken under the wing of Leonard Friedman rather than Tom Anderson? It's an intriguing thought. I don't know much about the classical scene in Scotland, but I do know that it has never produced a world-beating violinist. There's certainly evidence – in Aly's playing of slow airs, in his ability to master devilishly difficult traditional pieces without apparent strain, and in the ease with which he can rapidly absorb different sounds and stylistic traits from all over the fiddling world – to support the view that he would have been a star in whichever school of music he pursued. It could have been jazz; it could have been Scott Skinner. He has shown that he can play both of those convincingly. But a central part of Aly's musical existence is that 'the music must relate to your own experience'. If it doesn't, he argues, it is worthless. That's why

American music, which he heard so much of as a child, sits so comfortably on his fiddle. It comes as naturally to him as his native reels. During his teens and early twenties, he played more American music than Shetland music. It's part of his experience.

'They liked hoe-downs and that kind of thing in Shetland. American music was a familiar sound to them – it wasn't a foreign sound. Virtually every good American record that featured fiddle music would find its way to Shetland. Somebody would bring it back. It's the same today. If I think I've found a new guitarist in America and I meet a guy from the island of Whalsay, he'll have the record already.'

There was much speculation in 1984 when Aly Bain began work on his first solo album. He had been touring with the Boys of the Lough for twelve years, performing a repertoire that leaned heavily towards Irish music. What, we wondered, would he come up with on a solo album, where he had total freedom to choose the music he loved best of all and the musicians to play it?

He surprised everybody. He headed straight for Shetland, rustled up his old pals Willie Johnson on guitar and Violet Tulloch on piano, along with young May Gair on bass, and finally came up with an album that was overwhelmingly traditional Shetland in style and material. Of the twenty-nine tunes on *Aly Bain*, issued by Whirlie Records, no fewer than fifteen came from Shetland, with Ronald Cooper, Tom Anderson and Aly himself among the composers credited. There were five Irish tunes, three Scottish and five North American. There was one other: it was American in style, but had in fact been written as a Morris dance by the English folklorist Patrick Shuldham-Shaw.

It was called *Margaret's Waltz*, and it is one of the most entrancing pieces of music I have ever heard. In Aly's hands, it's one of those tunes you just want to listen to over and over again. Billy Connolly has already told of how, when he first heard Aly playing *Margaret's Waltz*, he couldn't get enough of it. It was on Connolly's advice that Aly decided to include it in the album.

Aly learned the tune from the American fiddler Jay Ungar. One night, at their Edinburgh home, Aly and Lucy invited their friend Shuldham-Shaw, together with the folklorist Hamish Henderson, round for a meal. Aly cooked a curry 'and then, of course, after a few drams Pat produced his accordion and I the fiddle, and with Hamish in good voice the scene was set. I had a feeling that *Margaret's Waltz* was a tune that Pat would like, so I began to play it for him. I was amazed when he joined in. When we finished, I asked him how he knew the tune, and to my embarrassment he explained that he had composed it many years before while in Shetland for a friend called Margaret Henderson, from the island of Unst, and named it *Margaret's Waltz*.'

Aly has since recorded two other tunes that Patrick Shuldham-Shaw wrote in Shetland – *Rosemary Brown* and *The Herra Boys*. 'I became friends with Pat during the '70s in Edinburgh while he was working on the Greig-Duncan collection of Aberdeenshire folksong. Pat was one of those rare collectors who, through his music, became a part of the community and enriched people's lives by leaving a few good tunes of his own behind. He and Peter Cooke played an important part in preserving our music by collecting tunes in Shetland that might never have survived otherwise.'

Margaret's Waltz became the tune that everybody wanted to hear again and again and again. There were so many requests for it that Robbie Shepherd had to impose strict rationing on his radio programme. And Aly only has to walk on to a stage for someone in the audience to shout out: *'Margaret's Waltz*, Aly!'

Aly recognises the tune's appeal, but doesn't regard it in any way as being a *pièce de résistance*. 'I learned it from Jay Ungar, who is a great waltz player, a great fiddler and a great musician. I learned it just the way he played it – I didn't do much to it. It's just that it's simple. Most of the great tunes are simple. You could try to write another *Margaret's Waltz* and you could write till you died, and you'd never get it. The actual notes in it, they're nothing – there are very few notes. You could play that tune if you were a five-year-old. I didn't want to do it on the album because it was so simple, but Billy finally had his way. I liked it as soon as I heard it, of course. I wouldn't have played it if I didn't. It's got that thing that *The Dark Island* has got. But what is it? I don't know. The first few notes are almost the same as Paul McCartney's *Mull of Kintyre*. Maybe that's part of the attraction.'

Whatever the reason, *Margaret's Waltz*, together with the definitive version of *Hanged Man's Reel*, sent sales of Aly's solo album soaring. There was thought of producing a single to aim at the pop charts – I, for one, was convinced that it would be a smash-hit – but Aly had other things on the go at the time, and it never happened.

Meanwhile, he is stuck with the tune, just as surely as Tammy Wynette is stuck with *Stand By Your Man*. 'I really think,' he says, 'that you can play all the complicated stuff you like, and people who are into music will appreciate it, but the ordinary man or woman who goes out to a concert would rather hear *Margaret's Waltz* than anything else.'

There's no doubt that Aly has a special affinity with the American waltz form. 'That's the nearest they get to a slow air. I love the tone and the style. Waltzes weren't rated when I was growing up. Nobody played them. If you played a waltz, it was a throwaway thing. But, like everything else, it's as subtle as you make it.

'Learning Scottish music when I was young is really what determined how I play the fiddle. It was learning the tone, learning to get a good tone. And that really came from slow airs and slow strathspeys. That's where you learn the tone. You'll find that very few Irish players get that kind of tone, and very few Americans get it. Tom Anderson understood that, and I understood it, because in Shetland I was listening to fiddlers like young Willie Hunter, who in his heyday had the finest tone of any player I've ever heard. So you would listen to Willie and understand what you were capable of getting out of the fiddle. That influenced me a great deal. Also, you had to use the bow in Scots music. You don't find that as much in Irish music. Our reels are pretty much an individual bow for an individual note, which is kind of like some bluegrass playing. When you hear someone like Mark O'Connor playing bluegrass music, it's much nearer Scots music than anything else.'

Aly continues: 'In Scots music, it's the rhythm that matters, not the amount of notes. Irish music is full of triplets and grace notes. In Scots music, there's less fancy

Tom and Aly play a Shetland reel for the great Irish fiddler Sean Maguire and Josephine Keegan in Yell on their first visit to Shetland

stuff with the fingers but much more urgency with the bow. There's more dynamic range. It's much more dignified and precise. It's very staccato, and you get that lovely cleanness in the music.

'Ironically, I learned a lot of that from an Irishman – Sean Maguire, who plays in a Northern Irish style which is similar to Scots music. The Donegal style is nearest to our own, like the fiddlers in Altan, very staccato and forceful and driving all the time. The real fiddle tradition. A lot of Irish fiddle music I hear today is really copied from the pipes. The real Irish fiddling, for me, is the Donegal style, which wasn't influenced by other instruments but which has Scots music in it because the Donegal people were travelling to and from Scotland all the time. The older Donegal fiddlers were listening to Scott Skinner, so there was a big influence from Scotland. And that's the kind of fiddling I like because it's pure fiddle music.'

When Aly was first getting some brief but welcome spots on radio, he used to phone Tom Anderson in Shetland after the show, 'Tom had set ways on how you played something, and you never had to play it differently. I could never agree with that. If I played a Shetland tune on the radio too fast, or put in something that wasn't

Historic get-together at Bridge of Don before the first Keith Festival (1976). It was Tom Anderson's first meeting with the legendary J.F. Dickie ('The Modest Genius'), one of the great stylists of north-east fiddle music. Back row (left to right): Aly, Alex Green (tin whistler extraordinaire), Ivory Duncan, Verona Burgness, James Duncan, George Webster (fiddle maker), Alistair Hardie (son of Bill). Front: Bill Hardie, Mrs Dickie, 'JF' and Tom

there, then he would make it clear that he didn't like it, or he wished I'd done it another way. My answer to him was: well, you do it your way, and I'll do it mine. Because his way was just the way he'd invented himself from a whole lot of styles, and that's what I think fiddle music is – it's music that's made up from lots of other fiddle players. You hear something that you like in somebody's playing and, without realising it, you steal it from them. It sticks in your head, and you end up doing it. It's what you *pick* from players that makes you the fiddle player you are.

'Music is constantly changing. If everyone was to play everything exactly the same, it would be incredibly boring. Once you have got a good grounding – and that doesn't take long, probably about two or three years – you should do your own thing. I'm not saying that young musicians should tear the music to pieces, but within the music itself there's a great deal that you can do, and there are subtleties in there that only *you* can play. It's a shame if nobody hears you playing them because you're frightened somebody else might not like it. Music is really about imagination, about what you're hearing in your own head. I wouldn't like to be anyone's clone.

'I know that if I treated music as a job, and practised every day from nine o'clock in the morning till four in the afternoon, as some people do, the standard of my fiddle playing would go way up. Technically, I'd be able to do a lot more things. But that doesn't really interest me, and it never has. The only form of practice that I've done has been to play in sessions with other musicians. What interests me is not being technically better on the instrument but finding things within the music that are already there and that can make it better. Anybody who has got the ability to play the fiddle can do all the technical things if they spend enough time practising them. There isn't a tune in any of the music books that I couldn't learn to play. Say I wanted to do Scott Skinner's *The President*, which is a difficult piece. It might take me three weeks, but I could learn it. I'd far rather spend the time looking for tunes I like – tunes which might be a lot simpler. But to take tunes that are written in a complicated way and play them just for that reason wouldn't interest me unless I really liked the music.'

Aly takes a few pupils from time to time, and he rams home the message that 'fiddling is a very individual thing – it's a way of expressing who you are'. If the youngsters have professional aspirations, he warns them that music is only 50 per cent of the task. 'The other 50 per cent of it is getting work, doing your income tax, and so

The second Heritage of Scotland Summer School at Stirling University (1979) – an idea conceived in Aly's house in 1975 during a visit by Tom Anderson and Robert Innes, director of continuing education at Stirling. Tom is centre, front row, with Angus Grant and Aly on either side. Jean Redpath, who taught traditional singing, is at the window at the top of the picture. Spot a young Kathryn Tickell (third row, third from left).

Masterclass: Aly and Dave with pupils from St Mary's Primary School in Haddington, Scotland
(1991)

on. There's all that side of it. And it's what people don't see when they think about becoming a professional musician.'

Playing the music is the easy bit, he argues. 'But you have to have a certain kind of temperament to do it. I tell my pupils that they have to be prepared to put up with disappointments and things not going their way. You really have to be an optimist to get through it all.'

In August 1990, Aly Bain underlined his commitment to the new generation of musicians when he embarked on a Scottish concert tour with a motley crew of talented youngsters. The billing was 'Aly Bain and the Young Champions', the latter including a couple of fine fiddlers, Angie Smith and Russel Kostulin, the concertina whizz-kid Simon Thoumire, piper Martyn Bennett and the clarsach duo of Vicki Ferguson and Gail Ross. The ever-youthful Violet Tulloch joined the tour as accompanist. There were packed houses all the way, and Aly's Champions gained valuable exposure and experience. The Springthyme label later issued an album of the tour's highlights. Inevitably, *Margaret's Waltz* found its way on to this one as well.

And there were waltzes galore on Aly's second solo album, *Lonely Bird* (Whirlie), which appeared in 1992. Violet Tulloch, once again, was on piano for this one, but in a significant departure from the norm, Aly brought in the ex-Pentangle bass player Danny Thompson, together with the English guitarist Chris Newman.

Significantly, there was only one out-and-out Shetland track on the new album, and only one short Irish reel. Aly was definitely going through his waltz phase at the time, although none of the four examples quite had the mysterious, heart-tugging quality of *Margaret's*. There was a fair sprinkling, too, of Scots fiddle standards, like *Mrs Jamieson's Favourite*, the beautiful slow air which had once brought tears to Aly's father's eyes. Thompson's long, dark notes on double-bass created a very special atmosphere which seemed to inspire the fiddler to new heights of emotional intensity.

At the time of writing, plans were being laid for an album with Phil Cunningham. And, needless to say, Aly was restlessly dreaming up new ideas for television films. But while all of this has been going on, he has never lost contact with the small Scottish festivals which gave him his first break. He is an ardent supporter of the Traditional Music and Song Association of Scotland, which organised the Young Champions tour for him. The TMSA runs several superb little festivals in country towns, notably at Keith and Kirriemuir, and Aly can still be found at these events as an honoured guest when his other many commitments allow. 'They are for me the most enjoyable of all the festivals,' he says. 'There's no hype at them. They feel like a part of the music. When you go to Keith you get a sense of belonging. You feel you're in the right place to play this music, with the right people.'

At the same time, he welcomes the way in which traditional music has been brought out of its 'little box' and is even reaching today's rock audiences. The Edinburgh promoter Barry Wright, of Regular Music, organises Scotland's biggest rock shows, and during the 1980s he started quietly slipping Aly Bain and others on to

Fiddlers three: a Keith Festival session in 1980, with Alasdair Fraser, Davy Tulloch and Stewart Isbester (guitar)

the bill for some of his major open-air events, like the Big Day, for the Glasgow Year of Culture in 1990, when thousands of people gave Aly's traditional music as big a roar as anybody got.

The man they were applauding, of course, is the man who, more than anyone else, has made traditional music acceptable and accessible and who, by his example, has shown that if you play it well enough, with honesty and soul, people will listen.

One of his greatest achievements has been to demolish the popularised myths of Scottish culture before the very eyes of his ain folk, to demonstrate that earlier generations of Scottish entertainers had got it terribly wrong in their obsession with tartan-clad caricature. There is still a lot of anger in Aly Bain about the travesties that were allowed to dominate Scotland's television and theatre for so long.

'Music has always given the Scots their identity,' he argues, 'but when I was a kid, nobody knew what our music was, so the identity wasn't there. Our identity is always going to hinge on our music and our culture, and if you don't preserve it then we will just become another European satellite. Even at the Shetland level, you need the music. Because that's your particular little identity, and you add all the little identities up to make the real meaning of being Scottish.'

That particular fight is by no means completely won. It still goes on. 'From day one,' as Aly puts it, 'it has been a case of battering down doors.'

The biggest door to give way, if not exactly to fall, has been as wide as the world. In Aly's view, 'our greatest achievement has been to put our native music on the international stage. Many people believe that folk music belongs in pubs and folk clubs, but we always maintained that our music should take its rightful place on the international stage. If we believe in our culture, we believe in ourselves as a nation. The fruition of that dream has made the million miles we have flown and endless years of travel worth it.

'The music will keep getting better. Who knows where the next generation will take the music? What's certain is that they'll do their own kind of thing with it, and they'll form new bands and be influenced by other music. And it will be great.'

Meanwhile, Aly promises to play until he drops. Into his busy schedule he will be trying to squeeze his two favourite pastimes – cooking curries and fishing the Shetland waters that he knows so well from his boyhood days.

'Being able to cook gives me a feeling of independence and self-sufficiency, but fishing is my greatest love outside music. To be in the open, empty hills of Shetland, surrounded by such beauty, fishing the fly on a hill loch, is too wonderful to describe. The sense of being at one with nature, without a human being in sight. The familiar sounds of the gulls and terns, the feel of the wind in my face, having time to think, waiting for that elusive wild fish, the flash of a golden belly in the clear water, and that great sense of belonging . . . it is, for me, the ultimate experience.'

I reckon he deserves some of those. His music has provided more than a few ultimate experiences for other people.

DISCOGRAPHY

BOYS OF THE LOUGH

The Boys of the Lough	LER 2086 Trailer	1973
Second Album	LER 2090 Trailer	1973
Recorded Live	TRA 296 Transatlantic	1975
Lochaber No More	TRA 311 Transatlantic	1975
The Piper's Broken Finger	TRA 333 Transatlantic	1976
Good Friends—Good Music	TRA 354 Transatlantic	1977
Wish You Were Here	TRA 359 Transatlantic	1978
Regrouped	12 TS 409 Topic	1980
In the Tradition	12 TS 422 Topic	1981
Open Road	12 TS 433 Topic	1983
Far from Home	Auk 001	1986
Welcoming Paddy Home	Lough 001	1986
Farewell and Remember Me	Lough 002	1987
Sweet Rural Shade	Lough 003	1988
Live at Carnegie Hall	Lough 004	1989
The Fair Hills of Ireland	Lough 005	1992

ALY BAIN

Aly Bain and Mike Whellans	LER 2022 Leader
Aly Bain	Whirlie 001
Down Home—Volume 1	LIFL 7011 Lismor
Down Home—Volume 2	LIFL 7012 Lismor
Aly Bain and Friends	TRAX 026 Greentrax
Aly Meets the Cajuns	LIFL 7017 Lismor
Aly Bain & The Young Champions	SPRCD 1032 Springthyme
The Shetland Sessions Volume 1	LCOM 7021 Lismor
The Shetland Sessions Volume 2	LCOM 7022 Lismor
Lonely Bird	Whirlie 002

Aly is also included on some early Shetland Recordings with Tom Anderson, including *The Silver Bow* (Topic 12TS281), and has had guest appearances on albums by Eddi Reader, Hue & Cry, Fish and Richard Thompson.